P9-DUV-518

**Planned Variation
in Education**

*Brookings Studies in*

# SOCIAL EXPERIMENTATION

*Editors:* ALICE M. RIVLIN
P. MICHAEL TIMPANE

# Planned Variation in Education: Should We Give Up or Try Harder?

*Contributors:* Alice M. Rivlin and P. Michael Timpane

Richard F. Elmore

Garry L. McDaniels

David P. Weikart and Bernard A. Banet

Lois-ellin Datta

Marshall S. Smith

Carol VanDeusen Lukas

David K. Cohen

The Brookings Institution
Washington, D.C.

*Library of Congress Cataloging in Publication Data:*

Main entry under title:

Planned variation in education—should we give up or try harder?

  (Studies in social experimentation; 3 )
  Papers prepared for a conference held April, 1973, sponsored
    by the Brookings Panel on Social Experimentation.
  Includes bibliographical references and index.

 1. Compensatory education—Evaluation—Congresses.
 2. Federal aid to education—United States—Congresses.
 3. Project Head Start—Congresses.
 4. Project Follow Through—Congresses.
 I. Rivlin, Alice M.
 II. Timpane, P. Michael, 1934–
 III. Brookings Institution, Washington, D.C. Panel on Social
     Experimentation.
 IV. Series.
LC 4091.P52    371.9′67    75-5151
ISBN 0-8157-7480-X
ISBN 0-8157-7479-6  pbk.


9 8 7 6 5 4 3 2 1

THE BROOKINGS INSTITUTION is an independent organization devoted to nonpartisan research, education, and publication in economics government, foreign policy, and the social sciences generally. Its principal purposes are to aid in the development of sound public policies and to promote public understanding of issues of national importance.

The Institution was founded on December 8, 1927, to merge the activities of the Institute for Government Research, founded in 1916, the Institute of Economics, founded in 1922, and the Robert Brookings Graduate School of Economics and Government, founded in 1924.

The Board of Trustees is responsible for the general administration of the Institution, while the immediate direction of the policies, program, and staff is vested in the President, assisted by an advisory committee of the officers and staff. The by-laws of the Institution state: "It is the function of the Trustees to make possible the conduct of scientific research, and publication, under the most favorable conditions, and to safeguard the independence of the research staff in the pursuit of their studies and in the publication of the results of such studies. It is not a part of their function to determine, control, or influence the conduct of particular investigations or the conclusions reached."

The President bears final responsibility for the decision to publish a manuscript as a Brookings book. In reaching his judgment on the competence, accuracy, and objectivity of each study, the President is advised by the director of the appropriate research program and weighs the views of a panel of expert outside readers who report to him in confidence on the quality of the work. Publication of a work signifies that it is deemed a competent treatment worthy of public consideration but does not imply endorsement of conclusions or recommendations.

The Institution maintains its position of neutrality on issues of public policy in order to safeguard the intellectual freedom of the staff. Hence interpretations or conclusions in Brookings publications should be understood to be solely those of the authors and should not be attributed to the Institution, to its trustees, officers, or other staff members, or to the organizations that support its research.

64349

# Foreword

In the 1960s the federal government's involvement with the nation's education system changed dramatically in two respects. First, priority was given to improving the education of children from low income families. Federal funds flowed to local communities to support compensatory education projects designed to overcome the deprivation suffered by the children of the poor and to improve their chances of escaping from poverty in later life. Second, the federal government began to insist that the education projects it financed be evaluated and that efforts be made to find out which education methods were the most successful.

Both these emphases were reflected in the launching of two related programs in the late 1960s: Follow Through and Head Start Planned Variation. Both were "planned variation" programs, under which local communities were invited to design, carry out, and appraise various approaches to improving the education of poor children in the preschool years or in the elementary grades. Hopes were high that, on the basis of systematic examination of alternative techniques, planned variation would lead to substantial improvement in the effectiveness of early education for children.

Although all the results are not yet in, it is already clear that much less was learned from planned variation that had been hoped. No one variation emerged as significantly superior to the others and no firm conclusions could be drawn about the relative effectiveness of methods of improving the education of poor children. What went wrong? Were the planned variations poorly designed, poorly executed, or poorly evaluated? Or was the whole idea of planned variation naive in the first place?

To answer these questions, the Brookings Panel on Social Experimentation (a list of whose members appears on page xiv) sponsored a conference of experts in April 1973 on the planned variation experience. The

vii

participants in the conference consisted of federal and local officials and scholars who had been involved in planning, executing, and evaluating planned variation programs; they are listed, with their affiliations at the time of the conference, on pages 177–78. The group came together to examine what they had learned about the planned variation technique and to assess its effectiveness in education.

This volume brings together papers prepared for the conference. In the first chapter, Alice M. Rivlin and P. Michael Timpane explain the planned variation technique and summarize the main conclusions of the conference. The next four chapters discuss the Follow Through program; these are followed by three chapters dealing with the Head Start Planned Variation program. The last two chapters draw on the experience with both programs and attempt to draw lessons for the future.

Among the contributors, Richard F. Elmore is grateful for the help of many people associated with the Follow Through program, especially Robert L. Egbert, its director. Lois-ellin Datta is indebted to Jenny Klein, Dick Orton, Dick Armstrong, Emerson Elliott, and Michael Timpane for reviewing her paper. Carol VanDeusen Lukas's paper is based on data collected under a grant from the Office of Child Development in the U.S. Department of Health, Education, and Welfare. David K. Cohen's research was supported by the Huron Institute and a grant from the Carnegie Corporation of New York to the Center for Educational Policy Research.

Both Mrs. Rivlin and Mr. Timpane were Brookings senior fellows at the time this volume was prepared. They are grateful to Deborah Du-Bourdieu and Nora Krasney, who provided research assistance; to Evelyn P. Fisher, who checked the manuscript for factual accuracy; and to Shirley Hornbuckle, who provided secretarial support. Alice M. Carroll edited the manuscript for publication, and the index was prepared by Florence Robinson.

This is the third book in the Brookings series of Studies in Social Experimentation. The series, which is under the guidance of the Brookings Panel on Social Experimentation and is supported by a grant from the Edna McConnell Clark Foundation, assesses the usefulness of experiments in increasing knowledge about the effects of domestic social policies and programs of the federal government. The research in social experimentation is conducted as part of the Brookings Economic Studies program, which is directed by Joseph A. Pechman.

The views expressed in this book are solely those of the authors and should not be attributed to the persons or organizations whose assistance is acknowledged above, to the Edna McConnell Clark Foundation, or to the trustees, officers, or other staff members of the Brookings Institution.

KERMIT GORDON
*President*

*April 1975*
*Washington, D.C.*

# Contents

xi

xii

## Tables

## Figure

ALICE M. RIVLIN

P. MICHAEL TIMPANE

# Planned Variation in Education: An Assessment

In the late 1960s two federal programs—Follow Through and Head Start Planned Variation—were launched with high hopes and ambitious, albeit somewhat conflicting, objectives. Both reflected faith in compensatory education—the belief that the lives and success of children from deprived homes could be significantly enhanced if the children were offered special school programs at an early age. Both also reflected uncertainties about how best to carry out social programs, and hope that experience gained from a variety of approaches could help to lessen the uncertainties.

Political leaders, if not scholars, for a fleeting time in 1964 and 1965 had seemed confident that quick, dramatic, and lasting results would come from federal programs to aid the poor, especially to provide enriched education for poor children. The Head Start program, enthusiastically launched in 1965 with the general notion that preschool education would help disadvantaged children succeed in kindergarten and first grade, paid little explicit attention to what kind of preschool curriculum was most likely to be effective or how success was to be measured. Almost immediately it became apparent that several very different approaches to preschool education were available and that no one knew how they compared in effectiveness. The definition of effectiveness was not a matter of universal agreement, and few measures were commonly accepted. Moreover, little evidence existed that gains attributed to preschool education, however these gains were measured, would last as the

1

children grew older and moved on through traditional elementary school classes.

Follow Through and Head Start Planned Variation were responses to these sobering realizations. Both were planned variation experiments— programs designed to try out different approaches to early childhood education in different places at the same time. Researchers who had developed particular approaches were paired with communities willing to try their models of early childhood education. Both the model sponsors and the communities in which the models were tried out had to agree to their being monitored and evaluated.

The two programs involved large numbers of people—federal, state, and local officials, school administrators, sponsors, parents, teachers, and children—and a substantial outpouring of effort, energy, and resources over several years. The results are not all in, and in the case of Follow Through will not be complete for several years, but most of the people associated with both programs would describe them as complex mixtures of success and failure. They would not all agree, however, on what constituted the successes and the failures.

For two days in April 1973 the Brookings Panel on Social Experimentation brought together some of the people who played key roles in both programs, including federal and local officials, sponsors, and evaluators—but, alas, no parents, children, or even teachers—to assess what they had learned from their collective experience. The conference was less an outside evaluation by disinterested observers, than an inside reappraisal by those who had lived through a joint effort and were attempting to sort out for themselves what it all meant.

The primary focus was not on substantive results—what had been proved or not proved about the comparative effectiveness of various curricula. Methods were the subject of the conference—what had been learned about how, or how not, to conduct large-scale field studies in education. The conferees were asked to address two questions from their respective perspectives. First, if they could run the two planned variation programs over again, what would they change or improve? Second, what should those who care about more effective education for poor children do in the future? Should they try to carry out better planned variation studies —with more time for development of models and measures, clearer definition and exposure of objectives, more scientific selection of sites and samples—or is the basic notion of planned variation in education faulty and doomed to irrelevance or failure? Should they give up or try harder?

## History of Follow Through

It would be pleasant to report that U.S. government officials surveyed the state of knowledge about the education of young children in the mid-1960s; identified several competing approaches to improving the performance of children from deprived homes, each of which appeared promising; decided that these approaches should be systematically tried out and compared; and then carefully and methodically set up the Follow Through program to accomplish these objectives. Unfortunately, it did not happen that way. Follow Through was "a programmatic and legislative afterthought."[1] Moreover, it began as a regular operating program, was shifted to a planned variation program, for reasons of expediency as much as conviction, and was rushed into the field too quickly and with conflicting objectives that never got fully sorted out.

It is difficult a decade later to reconstruct the hectic hopeful atmosphere of Washington in the early days of the War on Poverty when new programs to help the poor tumbled out of the White House and the Congress in rapid succession, and idealistic government officials worked frantically to get them started and confidently looked forward to quick and visible results. The launching of the Head Start program was typical of the spirit of the era. The idea for Head Start grew out of the twin perceptions, emphasized by prominent educational researchers, that children learned extremely rapidly in the early years of life, and that children from deprived homes fell behind their middle-class age mates in the preschool years. Poor children were already at a significant disadvantage in cognitive skills by the time they reached kindergarten or first grade. Those eager to find effective ways of improving the life chances of the poor felt that special preschool programs for deprived children would give them a head start, compensate for the vocabulary and cognitive skills that middle-class children learned at home, and enable them to function more effectively as they moved through the public schools.

The Head Start idea was not tried out methodically on a small scale to see how it worked, but was immediately translated into a large-scale national venture. In the summer of 1965, a few months after the idea first surfaced, half a million children were enrolled in Head Start. School-

1. Phrase used by Robert L. Egbert at the April 1973 conference of the Brookings Panel on Social Experimentation.

year programs were begun for smaller numbers of children the following fall.

Since results were expected to be immediately evident, instant mounting of programs was followed by instant evaluation. Those who hoped for dramatic evidence of quick success, however, were disappointed by the evaluations of Head Start that began to appear in 1966. Although the studies showed that Head Start children made substantial gains in IQ tests and other measures while they were in the program, these gains apparently faded out when the children entered regular school. The fadeout phenomenon was greeted by opponents of the War on Poverty as evidence that Head Start was a failure and by proponents as evidence that Head Start was not enough, that the initial gains achieved by the preschool program must be reinforced by a program of compensatory education for the same children in the early grades of school. Hence in 1967 President Lyndon Johnson proposed the Follow Through program to build on Head Start gains by providing continuing help to Head Start children as they entered regular school.

Follow Through was not originally conceived as a research or experimental program, except in the sense that all the War on Poverty programs were new and untried. It was to be an operating program providing additional compensatory education in kindergarten and the first three grades of elementary school for children coming out of Head Start. Pilot projects were started in the school year 1967–68 and a substantial expansion was anticipated for the following year.

Meanwhile, some government officials were becoming increasingly aware of how little was really known about effective methods of enhancing the educational performance of deprived children or, indeed, how that performance could best be measured. Education researchers, mostly in universities, seemed to have widely differing theories about why and in what sense poor children fell behind, and correspondingly different views about what ought to be done about it. Some officials, especially program planners and evaluators, began advocating planned variation in federally supported compensatory education programs. Their idea was to use the programs not just to serve children, but also as a vehicle for systematically trying out different ways of serving children and comparing the results. While hardly anyone thought it was appropriate for the federal government to dictate what curricula or methods ought to be used in local schools, even under federally financed programs, there was strong support for federal efforts to help communities to make more informed choices by fostering planned variation experiments and making the results widely available. When funds for a large-scale Follow Through program failed to materialize, advocates of planned variation quickly pointed out that a small program could still be highly useful as a vehicle for planned variation. It was thus decided to use Follow Through to try out varying approaches to early childhood education and evaluate the results.

Once this decision was taken, early in 1968, a frantic effort was made to get the planned variation program set up quickly so that the field operations could begin when school opened the following fall. Education researchers with promising approaches to early childhood education (some in preliminary stages of formulation) were invited to describe their education models and to become sponsors of the models in the Follow Through program. Selected communities were then invited to participate in the program and to choose the sponsor whose model they would like to implement. The Stanford Research Institute was selected to carry the major burden of evaluation design and data collection for the program.

By the fall of 1968 twelve sponsors were each working in one or more communities (most sponsors worked in several communities; a few large cities worked with several sponsors) and the first cohort of kindergarten and first-grade children was enrolled in the program. In the following three years, additional cohorts, sponsors, and communities were added, while the earlier ones continued in the program.

### The Follow Through Models

The twelve Follow Through models chosen in 1968 represented a broad range of promising educational practices. They included, for example, highly structured academic drill programs as well as programs where children decided what would be taught; programs that focused on cognitive development as well as those that centered on personal emotional growth; programs where parents played a significant role and programs where they did not. The ten models added in subsequent years were picked because they represented different sources of sponsorship —namely, state education agencies, minority institutions, and profit-making firms.[2]

2. Richard F. Elmore, "Design of the Follow Through Experiment," pp. 23–45, below.

One of the original Follow Through approaches is the Englemann-Becker Model,[3] which focuses on promoting skills and concepts essential to reading, arithmetic, and language achievement through rapid-fire drills, and uses reward and praise to encourage desired patterns of behavior. The Tucson Early Education Model[4] is aimed at developing language competence, broad intellectual skills, positive attitudes toward learning, and skills in reading and mathematics; it emphasizes positive reinforcement of children's interests. The High/Scope Model,[5] derived from Piagetian theory, fosters children's intellectual development through experimentation, exploration, and constant verbalization, with detailed plans for guidance by teachers and supervisors and a home-teaching program that involves parents. The Individualized Early Learning Program[6] bases its instruction in academic skills and concepts on careful diagnosis of each child's strengths and weaknesses, prescribed sequences of instructional materials, and positive reinforcement for success in learning. The Language Development (Bilingual) Education Approach,[7] using Spanish to teach mathematics, science, and social studies and treating English as a second language, relies on drills and culturally relevant materials and develops oral language prior to written language. The Mathemagenic Activities Program[8] emphasizes learning-by-doing, using positive reinforcement to encourage children to solve problems which are designed to assure advances in their understanding. In the Responsive Educational Program[9] children work at their own pace with equipment and games designed to develop problem-solving skills, sensory discrimination, expressiveness, and self-confidence. The Bank Street College of Education Approach[10]

3. Sponsored by University of Oregon; directed by Siegfried Englemann and Wesley C. Becker; began operating in 1968; 20 sites.

4. Sponsored by University of Arizona; directed by Joseph M. Fillerup; began operating in 1968; 20 sites.

5. Sponsored by High/Scope Educational Research Foundation, Ypsilanti, Mich.; directed by David P. Weikart; began operating in 1968; 10 sites.

6. Sponsored by University of Pittsburgh; directed by Lauren Resnick and Warren Shepler; began operating in 1968; 7 sites.

7. Sponsored by Southwest Educational Development Laboratory, Austin, Tex.; directed by Don H. Williams; began operating in 1968; 5 sites.

8. Sponsored by University of Georgia; directed by Charles Smock; began operating in 1968; 6 sites.

9. Sponsored by Far West Laboratory for Educational Research and Development, Berkeley, Calif.; directed by Dennis Thoms; began operating in 1968; 15 sites.

10. Sponsored by Bank Street College of Education; directed by Elizabeth C. Gilkeson; began operating in 1968; 14 sites.

stresses children's building positive images of themselves, with teachers helping in their development of plans and choices and their use of language to formulate ideas and express feelings. The EDC Open Education Program[11] encourages schools and teachers to experiment with diverse classroom practices in an effort to develop children's self-respect, respect for others, imagination, curiosity, persistence, openness to change, and ability to challenge ideas. In the Interdependent Learning Model[12] small-group instructional games allow children of different ability levels to teach one another and become relatively independent of the teacher; the games promote language development, reading ability, logic, and mathematical understanding. The Florida Parent Education Model[13] stresses the role of parents; mothers of Follow Through children are hired as teachers' aides in the classroom and work with other mothers in their homes; the curriculum is flexible and varies according to the needs of particular individuals and classes. In the Behavior Analysis Approach[14] teachers use tokens redeemable for special privileges as rewards for performance and individualized programmed materials to teach language, reading, writing, mathematics, and social skills; parents are hired to work as classroom aides and as tutors.

In 1969, seven additional models were added: the Hampton Institute Non-graded Model,[15] where formal grade lines are replaced by flexible forms of diagnostic and prescriptive teaching keyed to the individual needs and ethnic background of disadvantaged children; the Culturally Democratic Learning Environments Model,[16] using bilingual and bicultural materials that will enable children to function effectively in two cultures; Responsive Environments Corporation Early Childhood Model,[17] featuring special equipment, such as the Talking Typewriter, the Talking Page, and the Voice Mirror, that frees the teacher to spend more time

11. Sponsored by Education Development Center, Newton, Mass.; directed by George E. Hein; began operating in 1968; 10 sites.
12. Sponsored by New York University; directed by Donald Wolff and Jack Victor; began operating in 1968; 3 sites.
13. Sponsored by University of Florida; directed by Ira J. Gordon; began operating in 1968; 11 sites.
14. Sponsored by University of Kansas; directed by Donald Bushell, Jr.; began operating in 1968; 13 sites.
15. Sponsored by Hampton Institute; directed by Mary T. Christian; began operating in 1969; 5 sites.
16. Sponsored by University of California, Riverside; directed by Manuel Ramirez III; began operating in 1969; 1 site.
17. Sponsored by Responsive Environments Corp., Englewood Cliffs, N.J.; directed by Lorie Caudle; began operating in 1969; 1 site.

and energy working with individual pupils; the Cultural Linguistic Approach,[18] encouraging children from homes in which nonstandard English is spoken to build on the patterns of thought and language skills learned at home and to work together cooperatively without competition and rivalry; the Home-School Partnership: A Motivational Approach,[19] in which parents participate as teachers, students, and companions for their children, and as policymakers, so that the child views learning as desirable and nonthreatening; the Parent-supported Application of the Behavior-oriented Prescriptive Teaching Approach,[20] which helps parents to become tutors and to supplement and strengthen what is learned in school; and the California Process Model,[21] where the specific goals of each local program are determined by the community and the sponsor, so that all persons who touch the life of a child in home, school, and community will be involved in determining and improving his education.

Finally, three models were added in 1970 and 1971. The New School Approach[22] encourages children to follow their natural curiosity in initiating classroom activities and to take responsibility for their own learning at their own rate, while the teacher, aided by parents and older students, observes, offers suggestions, and assists pupils. The AFRAM Parent Implementation Approach[23] stresses the right of parents to participate in the education of their children, training them to become involved in community affairs and in the selection and development of classroom instructional program; it encourages community-based programs to deal with problems such as narcotics addiction and deteriorated housing that hinder education. The Role-Trade Model[24] allows parents, pupils, and other persons from the community to exchange roles to promote improved understanding and a true "community of learners";

18. Sponsored by Northeastern Illinois University; directed by Nancy L. Arnez and Clara Holton; began operating in 1969; 6 sites.

19. Sponsored by Southern University and A.&M. College; directed by Edward E. Johnson; began operating in 1969; 2 sites.

20. Sponsored by Georgia State University; directed by Walter L. Hodges; began operating in 1969; 2 sites.

21. Sponsored by California State Department of Education; directed by James Jordan; began operating in 1969; 6 sites.

22. Sponsored by University of North Dakota; directed by Vito Perrone; began operating in 1971; 4 sites.

23. Sponsored by AFRAM Associates, Inc., New York City; directed by Preston Wilcox; began operating in 1971; 9 sites.

24. Sponsored by Western Behavioral Sciences Institute, La Jolla, Calif.; directed by Stanley Crockett; began operating in 1970; 1 site.

in the classroom, instruction is carried out by a team consisting of a teacher, an instructional aide, and older children acting as teachers.

## Follow Through Results

By April 1973, when the Brookings conference was held, the planned variation program was in its sixth year and a decision had been made not to add any more new cohorts and to wind up the evaluation as soon as possible.

At the time of the conference the evaluation results from Follow Through were still preliminary and incomplete.[25] Reports on the program were scheduled to appear at intervals between 1973 and January 1977. It already seems highly doubtful, however, that the results will provide clear-cut indications that any one model is best. While there is some evidence that Follow Through children out-perform others on some measures, the preliminary results did not indicate that any one model was emerging as clearly superior to the others. They did suggest, however, that models with differing emphases produce differing results— models that emphasize acquisition of particular cognitive skills appeared able to deliver higher scores on tests reflecting these skills.

## Head Start Planned Variation

Head Start was of course begun before Follow Through; indeed, experience with that program prompted the decision that a Follow Through program was needed. Follow Through, in turn, was to some extent the instigator of the Head Start Planned Variation (HSPV) program.

The idea of trying out and comparing alternative Head Start curricula had advocates from the time the program was initiated, but the pressures of getting a large-scale service program started precluded planned variation in the first years of Head Start. In early 1969, however, the decision was made to invite a number of communities that were already participating in Follow Through to join a new Head Start

25. As Garry L. McDaniels stresses, the trouble with longitudinal studies is that they necessarily take a long time. See "Evaluation Problems in Follow Through," pp. 47–60, below.

Planned Variation program. If the community agreed, the Follow Through sponsor in the community would also sponsor a Head Start Planned Variation model. Thus it would be possible not only to compare a variety of curricula at the Head Start level, but also to follow children all the way through a preschool and early-grades curriculum designed by a single sponsor.

As with Follow Through the decision to launch Head Start Planned Variation was followed by intense pressure to get the program into the field by the opening of the next school year.[26] Eight Follow Through sponsors were initially chosen to sponsor HSPV models,[27] and three were added later.[28] One sponsor with no Follow Through experience was also added. The Enabler Model[29] allows each community to prescribe its own educational program, but all share a commitment to parent participation in policymaking, program planning, and classroom operation. A consultant from the Office of Child Development assists in development and implementation of all aspects of the model.

Three waves of about two thousand children each began HSPV in 1969, 1970, and 1971. About two-thirds of them were enrolled in the twelve sponsored models. The other third were enrolled in the regular Head Start program and served as a comparison group.

Head Start Planned Variation was a shorter, simpler program than Follow Through. By the time of the April 1973 conference the data generated by the preschool phase of the program were in the final stages of analysis and some results could be reported. Children in Head Start Planned Variation showed substantially greater test score gains than would have been expected if they had not been enrolled at all. They did not, however, do significantly better, on the average, than the comparison children in the regular Head Start program, nor did particular

26. See Lois-ellin Datta, "Design of the Head Start Planned Variation Experiment," pp. 79–99, below.

27. They were Bank Street College of Education Approach, with 5 sites; Behavior Analysis Approach, with 4 sites; High/Scope Model, with 5 sites; EDC Open Education Program, with 3 sites; Florida Parent Education Model, with 4 sites; Responsive Educational Program (directed by Glen Nimnicht), with 6 sites; Tucson Early Education Model, with 4 sites; and Englemann-Becker Model, with 4 sites.

28. They were Individualized Early Learning Program, with 2 sites; Interdependent Learning Model, with 1 site; and Responsive Environments Corp. Early Childhood Model, with 1 site.

29. Sponsored by U.S. Office of Human Development, Office of Child Development; directed by Jenny Klein; began operating in 1970; 5 sites.

Planned Variation models emerge as significantly better than others. Some models were associated with significantly higher scores on particular tests—one with substantial IQ gains—but when several output measures were considered, there were "no overall winners or losers."[30]

### The Wisdom of Hindsight

The Brookings conference participants had strong positive feelings about both the Follow Through and the HSPV experiences. "The amazing thing about both of the planned variation experiments was that they occurred and that thousands of people became deeply involved in making them work."[31]

For academic researchers and curriculum developers who became sponsors, Follow Through and HSPV were trials by the sword. Participation in the programs forced them out of the laboratory and into the classroom, where they faced the problem (often under extreme pressure) of translating theories and hypotheses into specific directions for teachers and children. Without question, the programs both hastened the development and elaboration of models that would otherwise have remained much longer on the drawing boards, and altered the models in the process. For program evaluators and policy analysts the programs also provided an invaluable education. They learned about the difficulties of doing social action research in the face of complex political and bureaucratic pressures. They found out, late and the hard way, about the costs that design flaws and compromises (for example, lack of random selection procedures) exact in the form of weak or uninterpretable results.

No one at the conference appeared to regret his participation in either of the programs or to feel that these efforts had been a waste of his time or the taxpayers' money. Yet the fact remains that definitive answers to questions about how best to improve the education of young children from deprived homes have not emerged from these programs, nor do they seem likely to do so. No model has come forth as robust in all or most situations. Nor does the analysis promise to yield definitive

---

30. See Marshall S. Smith, "Evaluation Findings in Head Start Planned Variation," pp. 101–11, below.

31. David P. Weikart and Bernard A. Banet. See "Model Design Problems in Follow Through," pp. 61–77, below.

prescriptions of the form: to improve outcome A, choose model B. At best, there have been a few clues of this nature.

The important question now is: what lessons can be drawn from the experience of Follow Through and Head Start Planned Variation that will improve the next round of efforts to learn about effectiveness of various approaches in education and increase the chances that more definitive prescriptions can be found in the future?

### Clarifying Objectives

There was a remarkable consensus among the participants on how, with hindsight, Follow Through and HSPV could have been improved. Lack of clear objectives had prevented the participants' knowing what was wanted. The objectives of public programs are normally complex and often fuzzy, and most programs could probably be improved by greater clarity in spelling out objectives. Nevertheless, in Head Start Planned Variation and especially in Follow Through the problem was extreme, and failure to clarify the objectives of the programs greatly reduced the chances of pursuing them effectively.

It was never made clear to all concerned that these programs were planned variation experiments whose primary purpose was to try out and evaluate different approaches to early education. Because Follow Through was originally conceived simply as a service program to provide compensatory education in the early grades that would reinforce and build on the gains of Head Start, it was subject to all the regulations on such matters as community participation in decision making that pertained to War on Poverty service programs. When smaller funds and an increased desire to evaluate different approaches to early childhood education caused federal policy officials to shift the ground rules and turn Follow Through into a planned variation experiment, many of the service program regulations were inappropriate—too much community altering of models, for example, would make the planned variation results impossible to interpret. Moreover, a planned variation program called for different time schedules (more time to develop the models, recruit, and train staff), different staffing patterns, and different evaluation techniques than did a service program. The shift in objectives was clear enough at the policymaking level, but it was not communicated to the Congress nor was it made clear to many of the lower-level federal, state, and local officials within whose ambit Follow Through was required to operate. Hence many of these officials continued to treat Follow Through like any other service program and to make decisions that hampered the planned variation objectives.[32]

Before the programs began, the question of their purpose should have been resolved. Was the purpose of the planned variation effort to test a variety of models individually (comparing each with regular Head Start or regular school) or to compare the models with each other, or both? Here again signals kept shifting and the confusion of different purposes hampered attainment of any. As late as 1971, for example, it was decided to emphasize comparison studies in Follow Through; but the analyses were greatly, if not fatally, hampered by previous evaluation design decisions.[33]

The model developers held diverse views about the aims of early education. Hence the objective of testing models individually would have implied the development of many sets of outcome measures, each appropriate to the goals of a particular model or group of models. A comparison of models would have required that some common measures be applied, at moments in time when the full program effects would be captured. The most useful strategy might have been to do both, developing measures appropriate to specific groups of models, but finding out how each model stacked up on the various criteria. It would then have been feasible not only to rate models on their own objectives, but to say how they rated in terms of the objectives of other models. It might then have been possible to give potential users and other interested parties the information that one model rated high on a particular set of outcomes and low on another set while the reverse was true of another model, and let them apply their own values in weighting the various measures.

In practice, while some sponsors attempted to define their objectives in specific terms and develop corresponding outcome measures, many had vague objectives, no specified criteria for effectiveness, and no firm idea of just when and how the hoped-for effects were to appear. During the course of the program, under the pressure of time and requirements

32. However, Robert L. Egbert pointed out at the Brookings conference that, since Follow Through had to abide by service program regulations, its models more closely approximated ones that could be incorporated into an operational national program than would otherwise have been the case. See also p. 29, below.

33. Remarks by Marian S. Stearns at the Brookings conference.

of national officials for comparative evaluation, the model sponsors acquiesced to a compromise battery of existing standardized tests as outcome measures. These, however, are ill adapted to distinguishing among curricula with different emphases.[34] Indeed, standardized tests are explicitly designed to give comparable measures of children's performance irrespective of what curriculum they have been exposed to, and hence are singularly ill suited for use as discriminators among curricula.

Finally, it should have been made clear whether the objective was to replicate the sponsors' models as exactly as possible in a variety of sites and observe the outcomes or whether local educators were to be allowed to change and adapt the sponsors' ideas to their needs. If the objective was to test the validity of the educational theories underlying each sponsor's model, then the models should have been carefully reproduced at each site and local alterations should have been discouraged. Sponsors should have had greater resources for training teachers and keeping in touch with their sites and more authority over the local programs. If the objective was to see what happened when local educators adapted a general idea, then less sponsor involvement would have been called for, but no conclusions would have been possible as to how the sponsor's model worked when implemented as originally intended.

Most of the conference participants would probably have opted, with hindsight, for increased efforts to ensure more faithful replication of the sponsor's model, although perfect replication is obviously both impossible and undesirable. Even more important, however, it is clear that the extent of implementation of the models in local sites should have been more accurately measured. The efforts made to monitor what actually happened in Follow Through and HSPV classrooms provide only crude estimations of the extent to which the models' operation conformed to their sponsors' intentions.[35] Hence, lack of knowledge about what actually went into the educational process in the various sites and classrooms makes it difficult to draw conclusions about the outcomes.

### More Time

Time in carrying out a complex assignment—especially one that involves several levels of government—always seems short. It is now clear that rushing the Follow Through and Head Start Planned Varia-

---

34. See pp. 103–04, below.

35. See Carol VanDeusen Lukas, "Problems in Implementing Head Start Planned Variation Models," pp. 113–25, below.

tion programs into the field with such rapidity was a serious mistake and greatly reduced the amount of information that could be gleaned from them.

More time and effort should have gone into development of the models before a large-scale field test was undertaken. The sponsors of the High/Scope Model candidly confess that it was far from ready for immediate implementation at the time they agreed to participate in Follow Through. They had been working with preschool children, had a general approach to early learning, but had not worked out a specific curriculum or set of materials for the first three grades of elementary school. Yet their model was more nearly ready for implementation than most of the others. Hence, the process of translating general ideas and philosophies of education into classroom practice occurred in the initial year of both Follow Through and HSPV; indeed, High/Scope's sponsors assert that their model was just reaching a state of full development after five years of Follow Through and HSPV experience.[36] Hence, it is not safe to base conclusions about the effects of fully developed models on the Follow Through and HSPV experience, especially in the first couple of years.

Even if the models had been more fully spelled out when field testing began, more time and effort should have been devoted to training teachers and to increasing the understanding of the model in the school system and the community. Participation in a workshop does not necessarily result in drastic changes in what the teacher actually does in the classroom.[37] The behavior patterns of teachers, administrators, and parents have been acquired and reinforced over a long period and cannot be altered by fiat or overnight.

More time and resources should have been devoted to developing outcome measures corresponding to both cognitive and noncognitive objectives of early education. Even in the cognitive domain, standardized tests may mask differences among curricula and they certainly tell nothing about other outcomes of the educational experience. Greater efforts should have been made, in Follow Through and Head Start Planned Variation, to find differences among models in the extent to which parents, teachers, and children enjoyed the school experience, in their impact on children's view of themselves or self-confidence or coping ability, or in children's ability to express feelings or share with each other. Few such

36. Page 62, below. At the Brookings conference such confessions led Harold Watts to term these early planned variations "purposive gropes."
37. Pages 63–64, below.

measures exist. They would have had to be developed for the purpose.

More time and effort should have gone into developing measures, monitoring what actually happened to the children in the programs, and measuring the extent to which sponsor models were implemented in local sites. Here again measures did not exist; it would have been necessary to create them.

### Improving the Experimental Design

Both Follow Through and Head Start Planned Variation departed in many ways from the conventional canons of experimental design. Some of these departures were inevitable and some might have been avoided.

In neither program were communities randomly assigned to models. In Follow Through a group of communities was selected to participate in the program, invited to join, and offered a choice of models. The communities chosen were those thought likely to be able to carry out successful projects.[38] In Head Start Planned Variation, communities were judgmentally selected from among those already participating in Follow Through and invited to participate in the new program. They did not have a choice of models, but had to accept the one already operating in their community.

Cohen suggests that using voluntary communities is not necessarily bad.[39] In the real world, decisions about education curricula are made at the local level. Since enactment of a federal program that dictated curricula seems extremely unlikely, the question of how a model would work in a community picked at random is not of much interest. The interesting policy question is what would happen in a community that chose to implement this particular model. Thus it is logical to try the models in communities that volunteer for them.

Ideally this reasoning leads to an experimental design in which a large number of communities are invited to volunteer and experimental communities are picked at random from the population of volunteers for each model. This procedure is expensive, however, and would raise hopes that could not possibly be fulfilled. Moreover, the population of volunteer communities, as Cohen points out, is not a static one. The

38. See p. 31, below.
39. See David K. Cohen, "The Value of Social Experiments," pp. 155–59, below.

number of volunteers for any particular model would increase if the results of the experiment were found to be positive.

There seemed to be no strong feelings among the conferees that models ought to have been randomly assigned to communities. However, some of the marked disadvantages of the system that was actually used could have been avoided. For both analytical and managerial reasons, it would have been preferable to have approximately equal numbers of sites per model. The system that was used gave some models too few sites for reliable inferences and some too many to be managed easily. Since Head Start Planned Variation was a subsample of Follow Through communities, the same problems persisted. Moreover, clustering of sites in particular regions or the association of particular models with particular population groups should have been avoided.

Although the participants in the conference did not insist that communities be chosen randomly, there was far stronger sentiment for random choice within communities of the groups that would receive the sponsors' treatments and those that would serve as comparisons. Ideally a control group should be as much like the treatment group as possible so that confounding influences are eliminated and differences in outcomes can be clearly associated with the treatment. The best way to ensure their similarity is to draw the two groups randomly from the same population. This is somewhat more difficult when the unit of treatment has to be a school or a classroom; but it would not have been impossible in large communities to draw treatment and comparison schools or classrooms from the population of such schools or classrooms serving low-income children. In fact, little effort was made to do this and control groups were often unsimilar to treatment groups (usually less disadvantaged). This fact made it hard to interpret the results.

On the other hand, comparison groups in these programs might have been drawn from a population of similar communities. If a comparison group were drawn from the same community, there would be some danger of contamination by the treatment. Teachers talk to each other; indeed, Follow Through and HSPV sponsors were often pressured to include other teachers in their workshops and training sessions.[40] Moreover, if community participation in decision making is part of the treatment, this participation can hardly be confined to one part of the community. Nevertheless, no two communities or their populations are really exactly alike. Hence it would have made sense to do both—to

40. See p. 51, below.

have two control groups for each project, one inside and one outside of the treatment community. This procedure, of course, would have been more costly than the one used.

Several participants expressed the view that both programs would have been better designed and executed if fewer models had been tested.[41] This would have made it possible to choose models that were in a more advanced stage of development as well as to have more sites per model. Moreover, with fewer models it might have been easier to find a set of outcome measures satisfactory for making comparative evaluations.

### Lessons for the Future

The strong consensus of the conferees that planned variation experiments of the future should have clearer objectives, more time, and cleaner statistical design was given concrete expression in a proposal for a five-stage process of development and testing of educational interventions.[42] The experiment would begin as a highly controlled investigation at a single site involving random assignment to control and treatment groups and careful observations of inputs and outcomes. If the intervention appeared to have appreciable positive effects under these conditions, a couple of years would then be devoted to developing it further, creating a training program for teachers and instruments for measuring the program's implementation and outcomes. The intervention would next be tried out under natural conditions in a small number of sites, close enough to the sponsor's home base to be supervised without great travel and communication costs, and curriculum, training procedures, and measuring instruments would be revised in the light of this experience. Not until after all of this development, small-scale testing, and revision had been successfully completed would a large-scale field test be undertaken to find out how the intervention works under a variety of conditions and with a variety of populations. In the final stage, full results of the field test and training would be disseminated to those who wanted to adopt the intervention in their own schools. The whole cycle, from initial experiment to dissemination of the field-test experience, would take ten to twelve years.

41. See p. 92, below.
42. See pp. 73–75, below.

Although the scheme is described from the point of view of the developer of a single model or intervention, it could be adapted to the simultaneous development, testing, and comparison of several competing interventions. In this case, outcome measures would be developed for each model—a set appropriate to the goals of model A and another appropriate to the goals of model B. But at least some of the measures would be applied to all models so that comparisons could be made—some of the model A measures would be used in model B, and vice versa. It would not be necessary for the funding agency to put weights in the various outcomes or make an overall judgment about the comparative value of A and B. It would suffice to make the results available so that local decision makers could choose and to offer training and assistance in the implementation of both models.

While many of the conferees disagreed on the details of such a process, there was a broad consensus that the basic aim was right—that finding more effective methods in education demands commitment of time and resources to a multistage process in which large-scale field testing of new models is a late stage, preceded by intensive development work on each model, small-scale testing, careful preparation for implementation, and special development of measuring instruments for both inputs and outcomes. The limited usefulness of various types of large-scale field studies in education leads Smith to similar conclusions.[43] He believes that the search for more effective educational treatments must focus on programs or comprehensive models (not on individual elements, such as pupil-teacher ratios). Such programs must be deliberately introduced and tested so that their effects can be isolated, but such field testing is unlikely to produce useful results unless more sensitive outcome measures are developed, more complete measures of implementation are created, and models have a theoretical base firm enough to permit specification of expected effects and criteria of success and failure—all of which takes a long-term commitment of energy and resources. In selecting models, however, Smith would look not only to the university and foundation-based developers; he would carefully survey natural variations to discover, describe, and elaborate new ideas developed in the field.[44]

There are clear obstacles, however, to carrying out any multi-

43. See Marshall S. Smith, "Design Strategies for Experimental Studies," pp. 127–46, below.
44. Ibid., pp. 141–42.

stage strategy. One is the difficulty of convincing funding agencies, and the legislatures that control their budgets, to make an investment (even an initial investment) in a sequence of stages that will not yield results useful to school decision makers for ten or twelve years.

Even if long-term funding is assured, it is difficult to keep the original developers of a model active and involved for many years. Scholars of creative bent may lose interest in the later stages of the process and, indeed, may not have the right talents for conducting field tests. Even if they do not lose interest, many will, in the normal course of events, take new jobs and move to other parts of the country. Local school commitments are also bound to change with elections and shifts in administrative personnel. Federal officials also shift jobs frequently, even during a single presidential administration, and a ten- to twelve-year program would be likely to span several administrations.

Even if a dedicated group of researchers, bureaucrats, and community leaders carries a multistage endeavor to completion, moreover, there is a more serious problem. The answers forthcoming may be to questions that are no longer being asked. Political and educational climates change drastically over a decade, and a strategy mapped out in 1974 may seem irrelevant when the results of field tests finally become available in 1984–86. Even over the five-year period between the inception of Follow Through as a planned variation experiment and the Brookings conference in 1973, drastic changes occurred in perceptions of what the important questions were and what educational interventions were likely to be successful. Some of these changes in questions hampered and reduced the usefulness of Follow Through evaluation. When Follow Through was started there was intense pressure for community involvement in decision making, and a strong feeling among black parents that "white middle-class" tests and standards were inappropriate for ghetto students and should be replaced. Both pressures had faded by the early 1970s. Perhaps even more significant, faith in the efficacy of curriculum changes declined over the period, partly as a result of the Follow Through and Head Start Planned Variation experiences. Many follow Through and HSPV sponsors began to doubt the importance of curriculum changes and to believe that a more fundamental revolution in the organization of schooling and the attitudes of school people might be necessary to bring about substantial improvement in student outcomes.[45]

45. See p. 76, below.

Hence, there are ample reasons for skepticism about a planned variation strategy even if major efforts were made to profit from the experience of Follow Through and Head Start Planned Variation. Can any nationally planned strategy do local schools much good? Coleman believes a shift in attention from the cognitive variables to the outcomes that school authorities actually regard as important (such as attendance and retention in school) would be a first step to useful results.[46] Can any method of social experimentation, however conscientiously carried out, contribute much to improving schooling? Cohen doubts that useful field experiments can be carried out, both because the essence of innovation is constant change (a new intervention does not hold still long enough for its effects to be measured), and because there is little reason to believe that policy decisions about education would reflect the results of experiments in any predictable manner, even if such results were available.[47] These doubts are reinforced by his fear that failures in education experimentation have been and probably will be blamed on the limitation of the subjects rather than the scholars.

Despite the legitimate skepticism of Coleman, Cohen, and others, most of the participants, perhaps reflecting the biases of their background, believed that planned variation efforts in education should not be abandoned, but should be more carefully planned and carried out. Mosteller points out that some kind of organized field trial of innovations is essential to prevent waste, because experience so far points to the conclusion that "most innovations don't work" and adoption of highly touted new methods without careful and systematic field trials has been and is a costly policy.[48] On balance, the conferees agreed that the preferred course was not to give up on planned variation in education, but to try harder, recognizing the pitfalls and building on the lessons of Follow Through and Head Start Planned Variation. Most of the participants looked forward to a day when more sensitive measuring instruments, more fully developed models, and more carefully designed field studies would make a major contribution to improving the effectiveness of education.

46. James Coleman, pp. 173–75, below.
47. See pp. 166–68, below.
48. Frederick Mosteller, pp. 169–72, below.

RICHARD F. ELMORE

# Design of the
# Follow Through Experiment

"The decision to use the very limited funds available for Follow Through . . . to initiate a program which will permit examination in depth of the consequence of different program approaches holds promise of inaugurating what could be literally a new era in governmental support for educational and social ventures, i.e., an era in which the knowledge and technical expertise of the educational specialist, the systems engineer, and the behavioral scientist are brought into harmony with the pluralistic value structure of our society."[1]

These were the expectations with which the Follow Through planned variation experiment was begun, and they seem in retrospect more than a little naive. Even though Follow Through and other attempts at social experimentation have not inaugurated a new era in governmental support for educational and social ventures, they do offer some important lessons in the use of the techniques of social science to solve social problems. What those lessons are is probably as much a matter of opinion as of fact, but there is a good deal to be gained from arguing about the lessons of experience. This brief attempt to discuss a number of important issues in the design and administration of Follow Through represents the view of one whose primary interest is in the role of evaluation techniques in the complex decision-making processes by which public policy is made.

In spite of an abundance of prescriptive advice on how social experiments ought to be designed and administered, there is a large gap be-

1. "Follow Through Budget and Organizational Staffing Requirements for FY 1968 ($15,000,000)," memorandum from John F. Hughes, U.S. Office of Education, Division of Compensatory Education, to Nolan Estes, associate commissioner for elementary and secondary education, Jan. 24, 1968.

23

tween good experimental method and actual evaluation practice.[2] This suggests that something more is involved in the conduct of social experimentation than simply knowing the rules of the game. Accounts of the early administration of the New Jersey Income Maintenance Experiment show clearly that the success of social experiments depends as much on artful planning and organizational capacity as it does on good methodology.[3] In education, large-scale experiments "require planning, careful execution, data-gathering, and analysis. We need not expect the first few to be carried out very well; we need experience."[4] Experience by itself, however, is not much help if it cannot be organized in such a way as to be useful in future attempts at experimentation.

### Constraints on Social Experimentation

The existing literature on social experimentation and educational evaluation suggests several constraints on the use of controlled experimentation as an educational evaluation technique. First, the byzantine complexity of the public policymaking process makes the conduct of social experiments extremely difficult. The decision to experiment and the definition of the policy question to be answered seem relatively straightforward and unencumbered by bureaucratic and congressional politics in efforts like the New Jersey Income Maintenance Experiment. But, as the early history of the Experimental Schools Program shows, a proposal to experiment may become hopelessly confused by bureaucratic politics long before it is ever translated into administrative practice.[5] The attempt in the

2. As argued in Donald Campbell, "Reforms as Experiments," *American Psychologist,* vol. 24 (April 1969), pp. 409–29; Glen Cain and Robinson Hollister, "The Methodology of Evaluating Social Action Programs," in Peter Rossi and Walter Williams (eds.), *Evaluating Social Action Programs: Theory, Practice, and Politics* (Seminar Press, 1972), pp. 109–37; and John Gilbert and Frederick Mosteller, "The Urgent Need for Experimentation," in Frederick Mosteller and Daniel P. Moynihan (eds.), *On Equality of Educational Opportunity* (Random House, 1972), pp. 371–83.

3. David Kershaw, "Issues in Income Maintenance Experiments," in Rossi and Williams (eds.), *Evaluating Social Action Programs,* pp. 221–45; and David Kershaw, "Administrative Issues in Income Maintenance Experimentation: Administering Experiments," in Larry Orr, Robinson Hollister, and Myron Lefcowitz (eds.), *Income Maintenance: Interdisciplinary Approaches to Research* (Markham, 1971), pp. 268–75.

4. Gilbert and Mosteller, "The Urgent Need for Experimentation," p. 377.

5. P. Michael Timpane, "Educational Experimentation in National Social Policy," *Harvard Educational Review,* vol. 40 (November 1970), pp. 560–62.

Follow Through program to construct an experiment under a congressional mandate that made no provision for experimentation is more like the latter than the former case.

Second, most important day-to-day decisions about the conduct of educational programs are made at the local level. The influence of the federal government over the affairs of local school systems is based on an elaborately contrived set of conventions that involve the consent of state and local educational officials, and, above all, preservation of the myth, if not the fact, of local control. In so far as large-scale educational experimentation requires centralized control, the decentralized structure of educational decision making can be considered a serious constraint.[6]

Third, as Suchman points out, "the conduct of an evaluation study itself constitutes a form of program activity—the planning and execution of evaluation studies require administrative resources."[7] Not the least of these resources is the time, energy, and intellectual capacity of program administrators and evaluators. Follow Through involves nearly 175 local school districts, about 75,000 children, and more than twenty treatments. Experiments of this scale may place too great a burden on the problem-solving capacity of finite human beings.

Finally, there is an irony in the fact that large-scale experiments in education were proposed at the very time when evaluations of educational programs and the results of the Equal Educational Opportunity Survey[8] were creating grave doubts about conventional notions of the relationship between school factors and measures of pupil achievement. Though large-scale experiments may have been designed precisely to remedy the weakness of the knowledge base in education, they in fact depended on some basic knowledge of at least a few promising relationships between controllable school factors and student outcomes. Perhaps large-scale field experiments ought to take place only as the final state of some more comprehensive, well-coordinated research strategy that attempts first to identify a few very specific causal relationships. The Follow Through case shows that it is by no means certain that weaknesses in the knowledge base can be resolved through large-scale experiments.

6. See David K. Cohen, "Politics and Research: The Evaluation of Social Action Programs in Education," *Review of Educational Research,* vol. 40 (April 1970), pp. 213–38.

7. Edward Suchman, *Evaluative Research: Principles and Practice in Public Service and Social Action Programs* (Russell Sage Foundation, 1967), p. 132.

8. James S. Coleman and others, *Equality of Educational Opportunity,* U.S. Department of Health, Education, and Welfare, Office of Education (1966).

This brief catalogue of constraints is enough to show why the decision-making process involved in the design and administration of large-scale educational experiments is likely to be quite complex. The following examination of this process in the Follow Through program is a search for useful lessons for the conduct of future large-scale experiments. The discussion covers five specific issues: (1) social service, social action, and experimentation; (2) selection of sites and assignment to treatments; (3) selection and specification of program models; (4) model implementation; and (5) the use of evaluation results.

## Social Service, Social Action, and Experimentation

Early in 1967 Lyndon Johnson asked Congress to authorize an amendment to the Economic Opportunity Act that would provide for extending Head Start type programs into the early grades.[9] His proposal had considerable political appeal. It was designed to capitalize on the immense popularity of the Head Start program at a time when other parts of the U.S. Office of Economic Opportunity's (OEO) community action program were coming under attack from state and local government officials who resented federal sponsorship of local community action agencies. It was also a direct response to the concern that the benefits accruing to disadvantaged preschool children as a result of their participation in Head Start were being dissipated by placing the children in substandard elementary schools. The new Follow Through program was to have all the essential features of Head Start—including extensive parental involvement; health, nutritional, and social services; and coordination with existing programs sponsored by local community action agencies. The critical difference between the two programs lay in the fact that Follow Through's target population was, ipso facto, in the established public school system, while Head Start's was not. Perhaps

9. In his State of the Union address, Johnson stated, "We should strengthen the Headstart program, begin it for children 3 years old, and maintain its educational momentum by following through in the early years." *Congressional Record,* vol. 113, pt. 1, 90 Cong. 1 sess. (1967), p. 37. In a later message, addressed exclusively to proposals for children and youth, he asked Congress to "preserve the hope and opportunity of Headstart by a 'followthrough' program in the early grades," adding that "to fulfill the rights of America's children to equal educational opportunity the benefits of Headstart must be carried through to the early grades." Ibid., vol. 113, pt. 3, p. 2882.

for this reason OEO agreed to delegate the administration of Follow Through to the U.S. Office of Education.[10]

Without waiting for congressional authorization of Follow Through, the program's administrators began a $2.8 million pilot program, involving 3,000 children in forty school districts during the 1967–68 school year, in expectation of a $120 million program in 1968–69 that would reach about 200,000 children. By late 1967, however, it was becoming clear that OEO's budget would not be increased enough to initiate a new program on the scale planned for Follow Through. When Congress finally passed the OEO appropriations bill in December 1967, the grim truth was that OEO would have to absorb a $10 million cut in existing levels of expenditure.

The budget cut was clearly the pivotal event in the development of Follow Through, for in the process of bargaining for the program's survival, Office of Education administrators and the Department of Health, Education, and Welfare staff had argued that Follow Through could be continued at a reduced budget level as an educational experiment to determine the most effective ways of educating disadvantaged children. In mid-December 1967, Robert Egbert, Follow Through's director, reported that funding for the program "appears to depend in large part on our ability to plan and carry through a program involving substantial planned variations among projects, which variations can be carefully evaluated in terms of the full range of Follow Through objectives." He continued, "We are eager to do this and are accepting the challenge of trying to bring it off despite fearful time pressure."[11]

While the budget cut may have provided the occasion for experimenting within Follow Through, it most certainly did not change Follow Through from a social action and social service program into an educational experiment. Those in the Office of Education with immediate responsibility for administering the program were strongly predisposed toward experimentation and indeed were enthusiastic about the idea. But their enthusiasm was based on a strictly instrumental view of the purpose of experimentation. "The decision was therefore made and

10. The texts of the delegation of authority and of the memorandum of understanding between the director of OEO and the U.S. commissioner of education are in *Examination of the War on Poverty,* Hearings before the Subcommittee on Employment, Manpower, and Poverty of the Senate Committee on Labor and Public Welfare, 90 Cong. 1 sess. (1967), pt. 9, pp. 2857–60.

11. Letter from Robert L. Egbert, director of Follow Through, to Gordon Klopf, dean of faculties, Bank Street College of Education, Dec. 14, 1967.

agreed to by OEO, HEW, USOE, and BOB [Bureau of the Budget] that Follow Through—*for the time being*—should be an experimental program *designed to produce information which would be useful 'when' the program was expanded to nationwide service proportions.*"[12] The administrators saw experimentation as a means of developing program techniques and sources of information that would be useful in embarking on a major educational intervention effort. The experimental phase of the program was a "holding action"—a means of keeping the program alive in the face of what was regarded as a temporary budget cutback. The object of the experiment was much less to discover systematic relationships between certain school factors and pupil outcomes than it was to develop a new intervention strategy for federal compensatory education programs. By agreeing to continue Follow Through as a planned variation experiment, program administrators did not substitute the goals of dispassionate, scientific inquiry for those of social action. The basic federal commitment to compensatory education was given and was not subject to experimental proof or disproof. Only specific programmatic techniques were to be the object of experimentation.

Nowhere are the consequences of this point of view more evident than in the willingness of Follow Through administrators to accept the constraints on experimentation entailed in the statutory requirements of the Economic Opportunity Act (EOA). They made no attempt to secure special legislative authority, or exemption from certain provisions of the EOA, in order to conduct an experiment. As a consequence, Follow Through is subject to the same statutory requirements as the other community action programs authorized under the EOA, including an allotment formula for program funds based on the relative incidence of poverty among states; a requirement that local community action agencies be involved in project planning; and a requirement that every project provide for substantial parent involvement. In addition, the administrative guidelines for the program, developed jointly by the Office of Education and OEO, call for "maximum feasible social, economic, and racial mixture of children"; "ample parent participation in classroom and other project activities"; and a "comprehensive" program of instructional, medical, dental, nutritional, psychological, social, and staff development services.[13] Finally, because Follow Through is a joint under-

12. Robert L. Egbert, "Follow Through" (1971; processed), p. 7. Emphasis added.

13. *Follow Through Program Manual* (U.S. Government Printing Office, 1972), pp. 4, 14, and 16.

taking involving OEO, the Office of Education, state departments of education, local education agencies, and local community action agencies, the initial process of organizing the program has been enormously complex.

Because no exemption was sought from the provisions of the EOA, it was established quite early in the program's history that the basic components of a comprehensive social action and social service program would be present in every Follow Through project; there would be no attempt at systematic variations in the kind or quantity of the basic social action and social service activities required by the act.[14] The variations in the curriculum models which comprised the experimental part of the program were to be confined within the bounds of the community action and social service activities that could not be controlled.

Since Follow Through's administrators regarded planned variation experimentation as simply a prelude to an expanded service program, there was a practical logic to their willing acceptance of the substantive policy constraints entailed in a social action and social service program. They were interested in determining the performance of a number of educational program models under conditions as similar as possible to those that would prevail in an expanded program. Eliminating the policy constraints imposed by the EOA would have created an artificial environment for testing instructional models and would have meant the loss of a great deal of practical administrative experience that would be useful in an expanded program.

Whatever the practical advantages, the policy constraints create fundamental problems of design and inference for experimentation. The dilemma might be stated as follows: If social services and parental involvement have a positive educational effect on children, then the effects of these unsystematically varied program components will be confounded with the effects of planned variations in educational programs. If, on the other hand, such services have no demonstrable educational effect and, hence, do not confound the effect of educational programs, it makes very little sense to include them as part of an educational program. Actually it is not possible to estimate the effect of unsystematically varied services in Follow Through because the only data that have been

14. The Follow Through guidelines are quite emphatic on this point. They are devoted almost exclusively to a description of the community action and social service components each project must have, with only perfunctory mention of curriculum variations.

collected on these services are suspect.[15] Evaluations of educational outcomes in Follow Through have simply ignored this problem, making no attempt to establish a causal link between social services and educational outcomes or to estimate the extent to which unsystematic variations in services are likely to affect measures of the performance of educational programs.

The problem raised by Follow Through seems to lie less in any inherent conflict between social action and experimentation than it does in the failure of policymakers and program administrators to specify the terms of an intervention in such a way that its effects can be studied. In Follow Through, this would have meant specifying that the sole purpose of the program would be to test the relative effects of a number of educational program models, and, without necessarily prejudging their value, eliminating other, unsystematically varied program components. What was lacking was not a strong predisposition toward experimentation on the part of Follow Through administrators, but rather the resources and possibly the will to pare down the program to the point where it was possible to concentrate only on the problem of the relative effects of alternative educational models. This failure is attributable largely to the belief, never borne out in fact, that experimentation was to be the first phase of a full-scale social action and social service program. If nothing else, then, the Follow Through case indicates that there is a good deal to be gained from a clear specification of the terms of an intervention—the identification of a central problem for experimentation.

### Selection of Sites and Assignment to Treatments

Random selection and assignment are fundamentally important to experimental design; yet, calculatedly nonrandom selection and assignment procedures were used in Follow Through. In mid-December 1967 the chief state school officers and OEO technical assistance officers in each state were requested by the U.S. Office of Education to nominate school districts for possible participation in the Follow Through program. From a list of 225 nominees, 51 districts were chosen as grantees, at a mid-January conference, by representatives from the Office of Edu-

15. The data come from project applications, specifying what a given community plans to do over the course of a school year, not from direct observation of local programs.

cation and OEO regional offices. The criteria used to select districts indicate that program administrators were less concerned with the effect of the selection process on the external validity of the results than they were with choosing districts with a high probability of success in the first year of the program. The criteria state, for example, that candidates are to be capable of mounting a comprehensive social service program in a relatively short period of time and willing to participate in an experiment not yet fully designed, and that they should have a well established, cooperative relationship with the local community action agency. The same selection process was repeated in two successive years—60 districts were added in 1969–70, and 12 more in 1970–71. No new districts have been chosen for Follow Through since 1970–71, although there has been an annual increase in the number of children in the program because of the addition of grade levels within sites.

At a hectic four-day meeting in Kansas City, Missouri, in late February 1968, districts were paired with program sponsors. In the first two days of the meeting the forty pilot districts were encouraged, but not required, to affiliate with a sponsor. In the remaining two days the other fifty newly selected districts were required, as a condition for participating in the program, to select a sponsor.

This process of selection and assignment is important, not because it represents a unique way of allocating federal funds or because it recommends itself for future experiments, but because it illustrates the extent to which selection and assignment procedures are based on quite deliberate and rational assessments of the conditions necessary for the success of a complex administrative undertaking. It also shows why random selection and assignment in large-scale educational experiments is likely to be enormously difficult to accomplish.

Faced with an educational system in which most important administrative decisions are made at the local level and in which state educational agencies, although relatively weak, are far more influential than federal agencies, federal program administrators must rely on persuasion, consultation, and monetary incentives to elicit the cooperation of state and local school officials. These conditions are hardly conducive to the kind of centralized control that is needed for randomized processes of selection and assignment. Yet the selection and assignment process of Follow Through is most likely the norm against which state and local school officials will judge more tightly controlled attempts at selection and assignment in the future.

Furthermore, there is a rationality in the Follow Through selection and assignment process that is easily overlooked by focusing simply on the mechanical application of the conventions of experimental design. At one point or another, virtually every political unit that might be in a position to influence the success or failure of the program—local school boards, local school administrators, parents, community action agencies, statewide professional associations, state education agencies— was included. In a situation where there is little or no hierarchical control, success or failure in a complex administrative endeavor might well be determined by the extent to which those capable of damaging a program can be involved in making decisions that would give them a stake in the program's success.

In this particular experiment, demands on local school systems were especially heavy, for there was little precedent at the time for allowing an outside organization to intervene in and restructure a part of the local school program. Hence, as a minimum condition for assuring that some good faith attempt would be made to implement a program model, it was necessary in the eyes of Follow Through administrators to offer local districts a free choice in the selection of a program model. Selection of models by the districts themselves, then, represents not only the reality of decentralized power in educational decision making but also a powerful incentive for districts to undertake the complex task of implementing a program model.

Incentives for good faith participation in large-scale experiments are especially important in securing adequate comparison groups. For Follow Through, the evaluator chose comparison groups from the non-Follow Through population within the same community or from a community that he judged to be similar to the Follow Through community. Treatment and comparison status was not randomly assigned. Regardless of the nature of the selection process, there is no strong incentive for the cooperation of comparison groups. For comparison groups that are within participating school districts, the chances of "contamination" among treatment and comparison groups are increased by the fact that local school administrators have no inclination or incentive to exclude certain schools from the presumed benefits of a program model. If comparison groups are in school districts other than those in which program models are being implemented, local school administrators are being asked, in effect, to suffer the inconvenience of periodic interview and testing without any of the presumed benefits of participating in the program.

The consequences of this purposely nonrandom selection and assignment process for the Follow Through evaluation are, of course, quite serious. They have been reviewed at length elsewhere and are noted here only briefly. First, the community's reasons for selecting a particular treatment will introduce an unknown and unmeasurable bias in the program's results. Second, the characteristics of the Follow Through models are confounded with a number of critical background variables: region, school entry level, prior preschool experience, and ethnicity, to name a few. Some models are concentrated in the North, others in the South; some in areas where strong preschool programs are readily available, some not; some in predominantly black population areas, some in Caucasian areas, some in Spanish-speaking areas. Third, there are large, systematic differences on important background variables between treatment and comparison groups. In most cases, these differences probably bias the results in the direction of showing no treatment effects.[16] Finally, for some models, there are not enough replications to make comparisons with other models reliable.

On the one hand, then, the selection and assignment procedures used in Follow Through are based on a quite rational assessment of the distribution of power in education and of incentives for participation under conditions of very weak centralized control. On the other hand the procedures result in inadequate comparison groups, insufficient replication of treatments, and confounded results, which make strong conclusions regarding program effects impossible. This bind between practical constraints and the requirements of experimental design will hamper future attempts at large-scale educational experimentation. It is probably possible to construct selection and assignment procedures, within these constraints, that will yield valid results. Indeed, it will have to be possible to do so, or advocates of social experimentation in education will find themselves in the untenable position of proposing an evaluative technique that will be useful only in the event of a major redistribution of power in educational decision making. More important, if the major purpose of experimentation is the development of useful programmatic techniques, the practical constraints discussed here may reflect one of the elements critical in the translation of experimental results to regular school programs. Policymakers are likely to be far more interested in how alternative program models perform under a

16. See Egbert, "Follow Through," p. 52; and John A. Emrick, Philip H. Sorensen, and Marian S. Stearns, *Interim Evaluation of the National Follow Through Program, 1969–71* (Stanford Research Institute, 1973), pp. 11–12.

close approximation of day-to-day conditions than under tightly controlled, contrived conditions.

Follow Through demonstrates something quite important about the conduct of social experiments in education: the conventions of experimental design, by themselves, are only a small part of what must be known in order to design adequate selection and assignment strategies. If the technique of experimentation is to become a routine feature of educational program evaluation, detailed methodological knowledge of what constitutes a well-constructed experiment must be supplemented by equally detailed knowledge of the political and administrative intricacies of the existing educational system. The combination of the two is essential both because it gives foreknowledge of the administrative complexities of experimentation and because it contributes to the usefulness of experimental results.

### Selection and Specification of Program Models

For social experiments, which seek to provide policy-relevant tests of the effects of a number of program models, the specification of treatments is of fundamental importance. Without detailed knowledge of the components of each program model, nothing (or very little) can be learned about how to translate experimental results into program activities.

Moreover, the difficulty of specifying program models in education is great—greater than was commonly appreciated when the planned variation experiments were first developed. During the past decade, conventional notions about the relationship between school factors and pupil outcomes have come under serious question. Basic knowledge about the effects of schooling may be so primitive as to make experiments with program models unrewarding. But it is unlikely that program development and evaluation in education will come to a standstill until basic research on schooling reveals more than is presently known about the relationship between school factors and student outcomes. The lack of basic knowledge on the effects of schooling is, and will continue to be, a constraint within which attempts at program development and evaluation will have to operate. Follow Through illustrates some of the consequences of operating within the limits imposed by a weak knowledge base.

Having decided that Follow Through should concentrate some of its limited resources on a planned variation experiment with program models, the Follow Through staff set about looking among researchers and practitioners for potential program sponsors. In January 1968, while participating school districts were being selected, twenty-six potential sponsors were invited to two meetings in Washington to discuss among themselves and with the Follow Through staff the idea of planned variation experimentation.[17] Among those invited were representatives of every conceivable school of thought and opinion on the subject of compensatory education. Some presented models based on adaptations of various theories of learning;[18] some advocated what could only be called general philosophies of schooling;[19] for some the idea of social action and community involvement in educational decision making superseded any concern for school programs;[20] and a good many others were so eclectic as to defy categorization.

The diversity of program models reflected a general confusion and lack of agreement among educational researchers and practitioners over what the important outcomes of schooling were and what features of schools and communities needed to be changed to bring about preferred outcomes. Not surprisingly, under these circumstances, there was some ambiguity as to what was meant by planned variation experimentation. In fact, there were at least two distinctly different ideas of planned variation experimentation expressed in the early stages of Follow Through. One approach, put before the 1967 White House Task Force on Child Development,[21] would have begun with a set of defined dimensions of variation and would have specified fairly clearly what variations were being tested. Systematic variations were suggested for such components of school structure as pupil–instructional staff ratio,

17. This account is based on U.S. Department of Health, Education, and Welfare, Office of Education, *Transcript of Proceedings: Follow Through Planning Meeting,* Jan. 5, 6, 26, and 27, 1968 (on file at Lyndon Baines Johnson Library, Austin, Texas).

18. Siegfried Englemann, University of Illinois; Donald Baer and Donald Bushell, University of Kansas; David Weikart, High/Scope Educational Research Foundation.

19. Elizabeth Gilkeson, Bank Street College of Education; Ronald Henderson, University of Arizona; Alan Leitman, Educational Development Center.

20. Kenneth Haskins, Morgan Elementary School, Washington, D.C.; Tom Levin, Albert Einstein College of Medicine; Anthony Ward, Harlem Block School.

21. David K. Cohen, "Variation in the Structural Features of School Programs" (Oct. 16, 1967; processed); and memorandum from Urie Bronfenbrenner to members of the Task Force on Child Development, Oct. 19, 1967.

teacher ability, socioeconomic mix of classrooms, extent and type of parent involvement in school program, and extent and type of non-parent, paraprofessional involvement.

The advantages of this approach were twofold. First, a planned variation experiment based on these dimensions of variation would have been, in effect, an expansion of existing research on the relationship between school structure variables and pupil outcomes—a more controlled test of some of the major findings of the Coleman study.[22] Second, variations in school structure, as opposed to variations in the substance of school program, would have the advantage of being "less dependent for their successful implementation upon the ability of a given school staff"; more "susceptible of implementation with relative consistency in a variety of situations"; and more "susceptible to evaluation, given the existing difficulties in measuring educational change."[23] It is impossible to say, of course, whether this approach would have worked any better than the one eventually adopted, but it undeniably had the initial advantage of simplicity in design and clarity in the definition of independent variables.

The idea of planned variation experimentation adopted by Follow Through was, of course, very different. Instead of specifying dimensions of variation and attempting to limit the experiment to those most susceptible to definition and replication, Follow Through administrators tried to select promising, innovative program models, leaving the question of how these models differed to a later time. This "all comers" approach to selection was based on no particular preconception on the part of Follow Through administrators of what the major dimensions of variation should be. Of the twenty-six potential sponsors who attended planning meetings, eighteen were invited to submit proposals for participation in the program; sixteen responded to the request; and twelve of the sixteen were finally selected. During the following years, ten more sponsors were added in an effort to give representation to three additional groups—state education agencies, minority colleges and research firms, and profit-making companies. The main criterion in selection of the first group of sponsors was whether they appeared to have an interesting idea for a program; for the later group, the criterion was whether a potential sponsor was in some sense "representative" of an important

22. Coleman and others, *Equality of Educational Opportunity.*
23. Cohen, "Variation in the Structural Features of School Programs."

or interesting educational constituency. As a result it is far from clear what the dimensions of variation are.

Even if concrete dimensions of variations in program were not specified, it might have been possible to approximate a fairly systematic evaluation design by defining each model in detailed operational terms and looking for naturally occurring variations among models, which could then be associated with expected outcomes. Follow Through discovered, however, quite early in the process of selecting program sponsors that none of the existing program models was sufficiently well developed to allow detailed operational descriptions at the outset.

It was obvious that despite the growing interest in this field and despite extensive publicity given various new programs, no one was fully prepared to move into the primary grades with a completely developed, radically different program.[24]

Follow Through's early evaluation planning also recognized the problem and the threat it posed to successful analysis of the planned variation:

Although many of those in institutions currently sponsoring Follow Through projects have been working for long periods in the field of early childhood education, we have been impressed, in our discussions during this year, with the extent to which they seem to operate on the basis of intuitive judgment rather than explicit principle. There is clear need for support which will enable those with long experience but still unsystematic knowledge to delineate more clearly the elements of their programs which they regard as essential to optimum development of the child. . . . The goal . . . is the development of operational procedures for the definition and measurement of program characteristics to which our measures must in the final analysis be related.[25]

Some of the research and development funds allocated to sponsors were to be used to provide the specification of models that was considered essential to a well-designed evaluation, but as late as February 1973 the program's evaluators were explaining that:

It is important to recognize that even if the number of significant effects were strikingly greater, we would still have difficulty interpreting how or why such results occurred because, at present, our current knowledge of the

24. Egbert, "Follow Through," p. 10.
25. "Follow Through Research, Development, and Evaluation Plans for Fiscal Year 1969–70," memorandum from John F. Hughes to Karl Hereford, director, Program Planning and Evaluation, Bureau of Elementary and Secondary Education, May 20, 1968.

treatment is confined almost exclusively to the sponsors' descriptions of them. . . . To interpret how and why results occur, we now need clear operational statements of what a sponsor does when he is installing and maintaining a project.[26]

It might be argued that the Follow Through program proves that it is possible to carry on something resembling an experimental evaluation of a number of program models *without* specifying the terms of the treatments. After all, results have been reported, and the latest analyses seem to indicate that a few models are more effective than others on certain outcome measures. On this basis, whether or not a model were precisely defined, it might be possible to say whether it works. As for determining what variations were represented, program models could be characterized as structured, unstructured, academic, informational, discovery oriented, and, when all else fails, eclectic. When this approach is considered as a means of interpreting program results, however, its limitations become apparent.

The results of several successive Follow Through evaluations have been reported, without a clear specification of program models, simply by associating outcomes with particular program labels or with the kind of broad, dichotomous descriptive categories noted above. Since these results simply associate certain effects with certain descriptive labels, policymakers and program administrators are left with no choice but to assume that each program model constitutes a "black box," whose contents are largely unspecified but whose effects are known to some degree. They cannot spell out some specified causal relationship of treatment and results, but rather must market black boxes. While this arrangement might appeal to program sponsors, who have a proprietary interest in their products, it is not a sophisticated application of social science to a problem of social policy. Presumably, since planned variation experiments are not simply exercises in product development, they should be designed to provide specific information that will be useful in structuring school programs, quite apart from indicating the superiority of one product over another. If the technique of planned variation experimentation is to become a routine feature of educational evaluation, some means ought to be developed for specifying dimensions of variation and for translating them into operational model descriptions.

26. Emrick and others, *Interim Evaluation of the National Follow Through Program,* p. xxxviii.

## Model Implementation

Being certain that a program model has actually been put into operation is an important, minimum condition for determining the effects of alternative models in planned variation experiments. If the evidence from experimentation is to be convincing, each treatment must be implemented in its essential respects, and for each there must be several essentially identical replications. These are considerations of design; they describe the assumptions an evaluator must make about the presence of a treatment in order to conclude that the results of his evaluation are, in fact, valid comparisons of program models. In addition, the results of planned variation experiments are meant to be used in new or revised educational programs; hence, it is important to learn something about the *process* of model implementation. If a given model raises particular difficulties, for example, those difficulties can point to the kind of administrative problems that might arise in disseminating the model beyond the bounds of the experiment. Evidence of this kind can also suggest the capacity of local school systems to adopt and execute the kind of innovations that planned variation models represent.

Implementing a program model in a number of diverse local settings is likely to be an enormously complex administrative task. Even assuming the model is fairly well defined (a tenuous assumption in light of the discussion above), it is unlikely that most administrators would have the capacity to deliver such a model with consistency to a number of school systems. And the way in which a program's implementation affects its results is uncertain. It has been suggested that the effects of even a well-implemented program innovation are apt to be quite modest:

Most innovations don't work, even when they are introduced with the best will in the world, are carefully thought out, and vigorously and expertly executed. . . . Why are educational innovations frequently ineffective? . . . When someone looks at a going school system and suggests that it be changed to make it better . . . he has two strikes against him. First, . . . the system is running now, and the proposed innovations can possibly reduce its effectiveness. Second, the people who formerly ran and are now running the school will have put a strong effort into doing what they can to make the system pay off well. So at best the change is only going to take up part of the slack between how well the system works now and the best it could do.[27]

27. Gilbert and Mosteller, "The Urgent Need for Experimentation," p. 379.

This reasoning, like the findings of previous research on the effects of schooling, suggests that expectations about the effects of program innovation should be quite modest. Additional reasons for modesty stem from the problems of institutional change:[28] All changes in on-going educational systems are fundamentally incremental; they represent not the difference between treatment and nontreatment, but rather the marginal effect of some complex change in an existing treatment. Thus any study of the effects of program innovation ought to take account of the incremental nature of change in educational institutions. In practical terms, this means that program models probably ought to be judged in terms of what was there before the innovation, what sorts of changes are entailed in the innovation, the extent to which the changes are actually implemented in any given case, and the relationship between changes and measures of outcome. One further complicating factor in any attempt at large-scale intervention in the established organizational routines of a number of school systems is the institutional resistance and selectivity in the acceptance of parts of the innovative program. This invites the question whether it is even possible to create several virtually identical replications of a program model, or whether, to the contrary, each replication will be some unique combination of the innovative program and whatever was there before.

Simply raising the problem of model implementation brings into question not only the ability to influence school outcomes through planned intervention but also the ability to apply the principle of replicability in large-scale social experiments that require institutional change. There is, in short, far more at stake in studies of implementation than simply establishing the presence or absence of an experimental treatment. Planned variation experiments are, perhaps more importantly, a test of a particular strategy of educational change and a specific technique of program evaluation. If evaluations of planned variation experiments were to indicate, for example, that it was impossible to implement program models consistently in a number of settings or that the level of implementation bore little or no relationship to differences in educational outcomes, then both the conception of educational change underlying planned variation experiments and use of the technique of large-scale experimentation as an evaluation tool would need to be reexamined.

Follow Through's administrators were aware of the difficulties of implementing a model when they began the experiment. They proposed a

28. Ibid.

series of community case studies that would detail the process of model implementation in a number of settings. The results of these case studies would then be used "to identify those variables that markedly affected program implementation" and "to work toward an integrative model which would describe the institutional changes associated with Follow Through and which might then be employed in data collection efforts at a larger number of sites."[29] In its execution, however, this plan of study became something quite different from an analysis of model implementation. It was transformed over time into a study to explain the relationship between parent participation and institutional change in school districts.[30] Little remains in the Follow Through evaluation that specifically addresses the problem of how well, and by what process, program models are implemented.

In neither Follow Through nor Head Start Planned Variation was an attempt made to structure a systematic study of implementation around a sequential set of problems: what was there before the innovation, to what extent were models implemented, and what was the relationship between level of implementation and outcomes? A number of observational techniques—including those developed expressly for planned variation experiments—might be used to detect changes in classroom behavior if a concerted attempt were made to observe classrooms *before* as well as after the introduction of a program innovation. The task of detecting hard-to-define institutional changes can be made easier if during the planning and development of an experiment the major actors in the implementation process are identified precisely and descriptive studies are constructed around the central problem of defining their role in the process.[31] Any study of implementation would, of course,

29. Stanford Research Institute, "Longitudinal Evaluation of Selected Features of the National Follow Through Program. Appendix F: Case Studies, 1969–70" (SRI, January 1971; processed), p. 3.

30. Stanford Research Institute, "Evaluation of the National Follow Through Program, 1969–71. Appendix E: Follow Through Community Studies" (SRI, August 1972; processed).

31. Two recent case studies of educational innovation and one classic application of role theory to the analysis of school organization indicate that there has been some methodological progress in this area. See Neal C. Gross, Joseph B. Giacquinta, and Marilyn Bernstein, *Implementing Organizational Innovations: A Sociological Analysis of Planned Change in Schools* (Basic Books, 1971); Louis M. Smith and Patricia M. Keith, *Anatomy of Educational Innovation: An Organizational Analysis of an Elementary School* (Wiley, 1971); and Neal Gross, Ward Mason, and Alexander McEachern, *Explorations in Role Analysis: Studies of the School Superintendency Role* (Wiley, 1958).

require a detailed prior knowledge of the essential components of what is to be implemented. From that, it should be possible to determine the level of implementation and the relationship between level of implementation and measures of outcome.

### The Use of Evaluation Results

The difficulties of design and analysis that have become apparent in the course of the Follow Through evaluation would seem to dictate caution in drawing policy-relevant conclusions from the evaluation results. Yet the U.S. Office of Education has proposed using Follow Through results immediately to restructure compensatory education programs. In February 1972 the Division of Compensatory Education in the Office of Education announced a plan to extend the sponsored model approach of Follow Through, over a five-year period, to the 16,000 school districts receiving assistance under Title I of the Elementary and Secondary Education Act.

In the fall of 1972, however, this plan was apparently superseded by another, whose object was to use incentive grants to encourage local districts to adopt successful, innovative compensatory programs. Follow Through was seen as only one among many possible sources of "validated" program models.[32] Clearly, there is a large gap between the desire of program administrators to control and shape compensatory programs and the capacity to produce validated program models. Indeed, if the results of planned variation in Follow Through follow the pattern of other research on the effects of schooling, it seems highly unlikely that anything like "validated" program models will be available for dissemination in the near future.

Moreover, it is unrealistic to expect that educational experimentation will ever produce unequivocal evidence of program effects. Under the best of circumstances, there will always be some fuzziness and uncertainty in the analysis and interpretation of results of large-scale educational experiments. Even if the design and administration of such experi-

---

32. Thomas C. Thomas and Meredith L. Robinson, "Analysis of Issues in the Implementation of a Program of Matching Incentive Grants, Part B of Title I ESEA," prepared for the U.S. Office of Education, Office of Program Planning and Evaluation, by the Educational Policy Research Center, Stanford Research Institute, Sept. 14, 1972.

ments can be improved, the constraints imposed by lack of centralized control and by the weakness of the knowledge base in education make it highly unlikely that results will be unambiguous. Rather than concentrating effort on strategies for disseminating results, time might better be spent determining what, if any, use can be made of ambiguous results.

Observing the ambiguity of program evaluations and the decidedly unscientific nature of the process of public decision making, a number of commentators have suggested the need for some institutionalized structure for discussing the meaning of evaluation results. One proposal would use evaluation results in an advocacy procedure similar to the court system, with open debate on the meaning of evaluation results for particular substantive policy questions and the development of "rules of evidence" to guide the use of these results.[33] Another would use an "adversary procedure so that an administrator could fairly hear the sides of a difficult question argued by prepared experts, with the help of his own experts to guide some part of the questioning."[34] The argument can be carried even further than this. It would be possible to provide for more than one analysis of evaluation results without markedly increasing the cost of the evaluation, since data collection is far more costly than data analysis. Continuing analyses of the data from the Coleman study[35] and the Westinghouse-Ohio evaluation of Head Start[36] have helped resolve the ambiguities of the data and answer important basic research questions on the effects of schooling.

## Conclusions

The problems of reconciling social service and social action with experimentation lie less in an inherent conflict between the two approaches than in the failure of program administrators and policymakers to specify the terms of an intervention in such a way that its effects can be

33. Kenneth Arrow's proposal, discussed by Cain and Hollister, "The Methodology of Evaluating Social Action Programs," pp. 135–36.

34. Gilbert and Mosteller, "The Urgent Need for Experimentation," p. 377.

35. Reported in Mosteller and Moynihan (eds.), *On Equality of Educational Opportunity*, and in Christopher S. Jencks and others, *Inequality: A Reassessment of the Effect of Family and Schooling in America* (Basic Books, 1972).

36. Marshall S. Smith and Joan S. Bissell, "Report Analysis: The Impact of Head Start," *Harvard Educational Review*, vol. 40 (February 1970), pp. 51–104.

studied. Advocacy of a general approach to solving an educational problem (for example, compensatory education), or of some specific solution may not be inconsistent with advocacy of controlled experimentation. In fact, given the level of effort required of all parties in an experiment to develop and implement a program model, it seems absurd to expect individuals to be detached and dispassionate about their work. The more important problem, in Follow Through, grew out of the program administrators' willing acceptance of policy constraints, which had the effect of confounding the results of systematic variations in an educational program with unsystematically varied social service and social action activities. This problem might be solved if the experiment were limited to comparing the relative effects of program models and if experimentation were not assumed to be the first phase of a large-scale operating program.

The conventions of experimental design, by themselves, comprise only a small part of the knowledge necessary to design adequate selection and assignment procedures for large-scale educational experiments. Both the usefulness of results and the capacity to administer large-scale experiments depend on a detailed, literal knowledge of how the existing educational system works. The usefulness of controlled experimentation as a technique of program evaluation depends in large part on how robust it is in the face of the constraints imposed by the decentralized structure of educational decision making. It is senseless to base an evaluation strategy on assumptions that depend on a major redistribution of power and a restructuring of relationships in the existing educational system. The design of large-scale experiments in general, and selection and assignment procedures in particular, depend on a detailed knowledge of the day-to-day administration of schools and of the kind of incentives necessary to insure the validity of comparisons between treatment and control groups.

The coherence of the design of large-scale experiments depends to a critical degree on the ability to specify dimensions of variation and to create clear, operational descriptions of the program models being tested. The "all comers" approach used in selecting program models for Follow Through has exposed the need for a better specification of dimensions of variation and the important components of program models. Policymakers and evaluators now face two alternatives for interpreting results—neither of which is very attractive. One is simply to associate results with program labels—the "black box" approach.

The other is to associate results with broad, abstract descriptive categories (structural, informational, open-framework, eclectic, and so on) that tell very little about actual variations in program content. The Follow Through experience suggests that before a large-scale experiment begins, a good deal of effort needs to be spent on specifying precisely what program variations are to be studied. The paucity of promising evidence in existing research on schooling does not bode well for future attempts at experimentation.

Detailed studies of the process of model implementation are essential to establishing the presence of a treatment and testing the view of educational change implicit in large-scale experimentation and dissemination of program models. To implement a program model with some consistency in diverse settings requires a very high level of administrative competence. Educational change is, by its very nature, incremental; the results of an attempt to implement a model may be some complex combination of the defined treatment and what was there before. Large-scale experiments must include some means of testing the notion of replicability.

Finally, the evidence from planned variation experiments and from research on schooling in general is not sufficient to provide the basis for plans to disseminate "validated" program models. Time might better be spent developing some institutional means of arguing about the policy relevance of ambiguous results. Experience now confirms what a number of the advocates of social experimentation have suggested; experiments do not necessarily produce self-evident prescriptions for policy. There is a clear need for an intermediate step between the reporting of results and their dissemination and use for policy purposes. Some form of adversary proceeding, coupled with continuing data analysis, probably ought to become a routine feature of social experiments.

GARRY L. McDANIELS

# Evaluation Problems
# in Follow Through

The Follow Through evaluation has a multitude of
goals, ranging from measuring the program's specific effects on children,
to describing issues of program delivery and implementation, to assessing community and institutional change. Nationally, the evaluation has
concentrated on those areas for which measures exist: child outcomes
(as measured by both cognitive and noncognitive tests) and effects on
parents and teachers (as assessed by questionnaires). The overall issue
is what the federal government's strategy for compensatory education
should be. Answers to a number of questions can help to resolve the
issue: Is the impact of Follow Through on parents and children greater
than the impact of regular schooling on comparable children? Do the
various educational strategies used in Follow Through have different
effects, and do the effects endure? Is there a relationship between the
extent of a given treatment's implementation and its impact? Are differences in impact among children related to such factors as their age,
socioeconomic status, and preschool experience? Are the interactions
between certain child characteristics and program characteristics generally the same for all program models?

The list of questions would have been much broader in the early
stages of the Follow Through evaluation, for the program's comprehensive nature, its relevance to important school issues, and the relatively generous financing of the evaluation encouraged high aspirations.
Contracts were let for the study of institutional change, community development, the impact of medical, dental, and nutritional factors, the
federal and local bureaucratic structures, and the effect of federal efforts
to bring about local change. A bewildering array of tests was planned
so that no opportunity would be missed. This is probably a ubiquitous

47

problem in social experimentation. Questions tend to proliferate, and limiting the inquiry becomes a major challenge to evaluators.

The proliferation was particularly heavy in Follow Through because of the large number of academic, community action, and public school personnel who had questions they wanted answered. The Follow Through staff worked much more closely with these stakeholders than with the policymakers who had conceived the study. The program was administered far below the policy-planning level in the bureaucracy. Moreover, as personnel in the policymaking units changed, new questions tended to be emphasized at the expense of the original policy questions.

Not until 1971 did it become clear that all the evaluation features that had gradually been approved for Follow Through could not be pursued. Priorities had to be established and, in the process, design strengths and weaknesses had to be reassessed.

### Design of the Experiment

The Follow Through strategy assumes that planned differences in curriculum can be translated into distinctive classroom atmospheres, which in turn produce distinctive child and teacher performance. Each sponsor in the planned variation experiment is expected to put its model of a well-defined, theoretically consistent approach to educating young children into operation in a number of communities.

The planned variation between the models of various sponsors is considered to be a more reliable means of assessment than natural variation. The utility of this planned variation design depends, however, on the extent of discrete variation possible.

Curriculum can be theory, books, teacher practices, student-teacher ratios, classroom organization, home involvement, teacher training, goals, values, and so on. Each curriculum combines some or all of these components in a way that stands in no clear relationship to the patterns of other curricula. The design has thus been a matter of continuing debate: What does each variation consist of, and how can its presence be determined or its effects measured? Are the variations planned, in the sense that they represent major alternative educational approaches, which should vary, one from another, in terms of process or outcome, in some predictable ways?

To the extent that such questions are not clearly answered (or are unanswerable), the planned variation design is of dubious methodological value. And yet, from a policy point of view, planned variation represents one of the greatest potential attractions of Follow Through—the chance to assess, or even rank, the "exalted claims" of educational reformers.

Whatever the problems of comparing treatment effects across sponsors, the Follow Through design still offers opportunities to determine the distinct effects of each treatment. Many sponsors offer their models at several of the 173 sites. Moreover, successive treatment groups each year provide a series of observations. The first cohort began the program in the 1969–70 school year, and four others in the following four years. At the outset, each cohort contained children entering at the kindergarten and first-grade levels who were to remain in the program through third grade.

Unfortunately, biases have been introduced at each stage, from the selection of models to the testing within cohorts, and the sample thus has serious problems. Because the sponsor's sites differ in number as well as in region, ethnicity, and urban or rural setting, many of the advantages of the replications for comparative purposes are lost. For example, most of the Florida Parent Education Model sites are in the South, most of the Responsive Educational Program sites in the North. Almost all of the sites where children enter first grade, in contrast with those where they enter state-supported kindergartens, are in the rural South. Most of the Bank Street College of Education sites are black, those of the Individualized Early Learning Program are primarily white, and those of the Language Development (Bilingual) Education Approach are in Spanish-speaking communities.[1] Furthermore, the number of sites per sponsor ranges from one to twenty.

In addition to the picture it provides of the elements of a curriculum, the Follow Through treatment provides a unique opportunity for studying children over a period of three or four years. But the question inevitably arises, how many years are enough? Even in Follow Through, with its longitudinal design and successive replications, four years is attacked as too restricted a treatment period; stopping the treatment at the end of the third grade as a time "when the problems are just beginning"; or any kind of testing that is not continued into the upper elementary grades and junior high as unrepresentative of a true estimate of the

1. See descriptions of the programs on pp. 6–9, above.

impact. Moreover, concluding the major testing with the third cohort is attacked as too early in the sponsors' community development to measure programs successfully. But the alternative in each instance would further lengthen the experiment, and length is a problem in itself. Because of the time required for treatments of five cohorts, Follow Through will fall in four presidential administrations. Not only will the policy study outlast presidents, the original policy planners, the program directors, and the program evaluators, but the treatments must be able to outlive their original sponsors. By 1973, three Follow Through models had changed institutional bases and in seven others the involvement of the creators had been either greatly reduced or lost entirely. This raises serious questions about the use of the longitudinal design in policy studies.

A small longitudinal intervention has certain limitations that a district-wide program would not suffer. Since it is an experiment, Follow Through usually exists in only one school in a district. In large metropolitan areas children move from school to school.[2] A child can enter a Follow Through school at any time, so that a Follow Through third-grade classroom may have children with one to four years of experience in the model. If the intervention covered all schools in a large geographic area, the children would move among classrooms that had the program. Children entering a model program probably need time to adjust to new routines, and the classroom program must also adjust to accommodate new students. Thus the model changes continually at each site.

### Design of the Evaluation

When the strategy for measuring Follow Through was being developed, a decision was made to include new, unstandardized instruments so that a broad range of student behavior could be documented. Since national norms were not available for these instruments, groups of comparison children were identified in each site. But children compa-

2. The 660 kindergarten children included in a sample from 29 Philadelphia schools in the 1968–69 school year had spread to 110 schools by the 1971–72 school year; Marshall Swift and George Spivack, "A Longitudinal Study of Behavioral Effectiveness, and the Emotional, Educational Development of Head Start and Follow Through Children" (Hahnemann Medical College, Philadelphia, 1972; processed).

rable to the Follow Through population were not always easy to identify. In some sites Follow Through serves all eligible children, so comparison children had to be sought in nearby districts, or, more often, among a more advantaged socioeconomic group. Where reasonably similar children were found in other districts, it has been difficult to retain the schools' cooperation. The comparison schools receive no Follow Through grants, and yet they are asked to offer access to their students, parents, and teachers for four years. Feedback does not provide any immediate incentive for them to remain a part of the sample, and they are increasingly reluctant to allow the collection of data.

School programming raises another problem. The Follow Through program is but one of hundreds of federal, state, and local programs of compensatory education. The children being compared are usually receiving Title I funds. They may also be participating in specialized programs in reading, mathematics, and sciences, so that children in Follow Through are often being compared with children in other intervention programs, rather than with children for whom no special programming is available.

There is a third problem resulting from Follow Through "seepage." In some schools, only a portion of the classrooms at any grade level are receiving Follow Through funds and services, and comparison groups are located in the same schools. However, it has become apparent that all the classes at a particular grade level use Follow Through equipment, and all faculty members generally attend sponsor workshops. The Follow Through program often serves as a model for organizing classrooms. Sponsors are usually glad to offer additional training workshops on their visits. This seepage is a positive indicator of the program's success, but the children being compared are receiving the same academic instruction as Follow Through children.

Measurement issues have plagued both the Head Start Planned Variation program and Follow Through. The basic problem is how to assess a variety of treatments with different goals. In the test and measurement field, both the validity of the content and the psychometric properties and assumptions underlying tests are points of disagreement. The Follow Through test battery, questionnaires, and surveys were modified a number of times before the spring of 1972, when it was decided that improvements in the tests were by no means worth the loss in comparability over time. At that time the Metropolitan Achievement Test and several noncognitive measures were planned as a core battery, to be used throughout the rest of the data collecting period. Since the studies were focused primarily on academic outcomes, the decision seemed appropriate.

Assessing several models, each with different goals, places a heavy burden on an evaluator. In Follow Through, the prime emphasis of a sponsor may be short-term achievement gains, or long-term changes in cognitive strategies, or altering the behavior of parents in their interactions with children, or modifying children's self-concept as a precursor to altering cognitive outcomes. Focusing an evaluation on one set of outcomes therefore places a few sponsors in an advantageous position. In the early years of the study the Follow Through staff tried to develop an instrument battery to meet all variations, designing specific items for each sponsor to be administered to all children (unfortunately, when the items were pooled, distinctions between treatments were masked). Cognitive tests were changed so as to be fairer to the population of Follow Through children, but the modification destroyed the comparability of the scores to national norms. Tests of noncognitive outcomes were developed, but none of the hodgepodge of instruments appears to be able to produce reliable results. In the later stages of the evaluation, the strategy has changed to focus on a few standardized tests of cognitive outcomes, and to experiment with a few tests of noncognitive outcomes.

What proves that a model is successful? How much difference between Follow Through and non-Follow Through pupils should be expected at the end of one year, two years, and so on? How much satisfaction should parents and teachers express if a program is to be considered a success? The answers to these questions depend upon how the measurements taken are interpreted and on the comparisons made. From a standardized achievement test, differences in outcome can be stated in terms of raw scores or adjusted score points, transformed scores (standardized or grade equivalents), or standard deviations in any of these metrics. The choice of metric is in part a function of the comparison that is to be made. For example, grade equivalents are generally based on previously established national norms and thus contain implicit comparisons to a larger population. With raw scores, comparisons should probably be restricted to the population being studied. Clearly there is no best comparison and thus no best metric. Because there are a number of different ways of looking at results, a set of criteria for success should be agreed upon at the beginning of a study in terms of the metric desired.

But what are the criteria for success? Is a model successful if, after four years, Follow Through children are six months behind grade level while other children are one year behind? Is a model successful if, after one year, Follow Through children are one-half a standard deviation above those they are being compared with, but, after four years, only one-sixth of a standard deviation ahead? How do expectations vary for different stages in the program? For example, must the difference be as large at the end of third grade as at the end of kindergarten? The answers to these questions are not obvious. However, if social experimentation is to be useful in guiding public policy, answers to these questions must be developed.

Follow Through's relationship with the Head Start Planned Variation longitudinal study is typical of the bureaucratic difficulties in coordinating efforts between two agencies. Because the Head Start study was set up with the longitudinal component in mind, the sites were chosen in communities with Follow Through programs. However, those in charge of the programs failed to ensure that an adequate sample of Head Start Planned Variation children entered Follow Through schools. As a result, the sample for the longitudinal study had to be developed after the fact from those sites where a large number of children had moved from the one program into the other.

Obviously any field experiment is subject to a variety of influences that the experimenter cannot control. While these events do not necessarily destroy an experiment, they can have a variety of effects on treatments, tests, and samples. One Follow Through site, for instance, had to be withdrawn from the evaluation because the school was flooded. Teacher strikes in Philadelphia delayed testing and have perhaps altered the impact of the program there. And desegregation of school systems has scattered children from Follow Through classrooms to dozens of regular elementary schools.

## Focus of the Evaluation

The Follow Through evaluation began as a sweepingly broad effort to collect data on children, teachers, and parents in most sites. To estimate the general effect of Follow Through, data were to be collected at the beginning and end of each cohort, with some intermediate testing for special purposes and to determine trends. This approach created extensive confusion about the purposes of the evaluation. The Follow Through evaluation was therefore reorganized into a series of specific studies.

In 1971, sponsors with fewer than three sites or an unrepresentative distribution of sites were eliminated from the Follow Through evaluation. In the first cohort, which had entered in 1969, five sponsors with three or four sites and two with five remained in the evaluation. The second cohort included eleven sponsors with three or four sites and five with five sites, and the third included eleven with three or four sites and ten with five. By the spring of 1972, base-line data had been collected on these sites. The cost was so astonishing (ten tons of materials and 2,200 people in the field were needed for a scaled-down effort in the spring of 1972) that the need for testing was reconsidered in terms of cost, effort, and knowledge gained. The eventual decision was to continue studies on the first three cohorts, to study only cities in the fourth, and to collect no data on the fifth.[3] On the first two cohorts, tests would be given only after the children had completed third grade.

For the third cohort, which had just begun, it was possible to include eleven sponsors and three hundred schools in the study. Each of the sponsors had had at least two years' prior experience at these schools before the third cohort children entered the classes, so their models should have been reasonably well implemented. The progress of the children in this cohort would be monitored at the end of each year, from kindergarten through third grade. Thus the third cohort sample combines the necessary elements for comparing models, both in overall effect at the end of the program and at each grade interval. The extensive intermediate testings not only permit model comparisons but also allow for a study of patterns of growth in each model from grade to grade.

### The Cities Study

The studies of six sponsors with sites in New York City and seven in Philadelphia provide a unique opportunity for sponsor comparison.

3. It was estimated that the cost of collecting and analyzing the data could approach $40 million if all possible data continued to be collected in the five cohorts.

Samples within a city, especially in Philadelphia, should have more common characteristics than samples from different cities and regions. Most of the sites for these two cities were retained in the first four cohorts to strengthen comparisons among sponsors within each city.

### The Summer Effects Study

Variations in children's backgrounds (particularly social class), it is currently argued, have a much greater impact on their school achievement than do variations in school resources. The range of variations in exposure to schooling through grade twelve is quite limited, and little is known about the difference in effects of exposure between the extremes of school and no school. One investigation of exposure to schooling as against no exposure during the summer months indicates that the difference in the rate of growth of achievement of poor and nonpoor children is greater over the summer months than during the school year.[4]

This finding suggests that schooling might be viewed as an equalizing experience for children. If participation in a summer program heightens the amount of retention from spring to fall, an extension of school— for example, summer school—might help to equalize the experience of poor children with that of richer children. The Follow Through evaluation called for children at three grade levels in Philadelphia and at one grade level in six other sites to take the Metropolitan Achievement Test in the spring and fall of 1972 and the spring of 1973, and for their parents to be interviewed to provide demographic information about the child's experiences over the summer.

The Philadelphia sample is being used to investigate relationships between home environment variables and summer growth, and the six others to assess the effects of a summer program. At the six sites, eligible Follow Through children were randomly assigned to summer programs and to control groups. From this experience have come some practical lessons in the difficulties of making random assignments. For example, the requirements for eligibility (parental interest and participation in Follow Through) must produce a large enough pool to leave a sufficient number of controls after summer program assignments. Furthermore, it is important to investigate competing programs in order

4. Donald P. Hayes and Judith Grether, "The School Year and Vacations: When Do Students Learn?" (revision of a paper presented at the Eastern Sociological Association convention, New York City, April 19, 1969).

to determine whether the controls have received treatments very similar to those of the experimental children. The study has shown that random assignment to treatment and control groups is possible in social experiments. Cooperation can be achieved at the local level if reasonable planning at the federal level is followed by extensive on-site explanation and encouragement.

## Head Start Longitudinal Study

One of the major purposes behind the introduction of planned variations in Head Start was to assess the combined impact on children who moved from Head Start Planned Variation into Follow Through. Because of sampling and attrition problems, the study was limited to fourteen sites. It includes two waves of children in the regular Head Start program as well as those in Planned Variation. Both groups were tested at the beginning and the end of their Head Start experience; with the Follow Through tests it will be possible to explore the effects of various combinations of preschool and elementary school experiences.

## Entering-First Study

In several states, primarily in the southeastern and southwestern regions where kindergartens are not publicly funded, Follow Through begins with the first grade. Thus within a cohort there are actually two different kinds of sites. Those that begin with grade one pose some major evaluation problems: many of them have recently added kindergarten, so that there are two streams of children in the same site; many of the original Follow Through classes and schools have been broken up by integration efforts; and sites are distributed unevenly by sponsor, region, or ethnic group.

Because those sites with children entering at the first grade were the first "graduating class" in the first cohort of Follow Through, many of them were retained in the evaluation sample. They were cut drastically, however, in the second and third cohorts (only those belonging to sponsors with at least two comparable sites were kept). The small number in the sample lowers confidence in the effects measured. However, these sites are unique not only in that children are normally six rather than five years of age when they enter the program, but the sites are primarily in the southeastern United States and primarily rural.

They could furnish evidence of any strong effect of these characteristics on the treatments.


## Interpretation of Interim Findings


Since the Follow Through evaluation spans seven years, at a minimum, it is hardly realistic to postpone reporting its results until the very end. But at what stage is it destructive to the evaluation to release findings? How should the data be presented? An honest presentation of short-term and interim results requires a complex explanation to guard against misinterpretation. The complexities involved limit considerably the audience that can understand the issues.

The data on the first year of the first cohort amply illustrate this problem; the experiment can readily be interpreted as a failure because Follow Through children's scores were no better than those of other children. But such a conclusion is not warranted, for the treatment and control groups were not necessarily comparable; the sponsors had had little time to implement their models; and there were not enough sites per sponsor to estimate effects adequately. These limiting conditions are very important, as the first-year findings on the third cohort illustrate. In this improved sample, with a number of sites per sponsor, several sponsors looked very strong at the end of the first year, while others did not (on the one achievement measure analyzed); the strongest were those who emphasize short-term achievement effects. If these data were highly publicized, two unwarranted conclusions would probably be reached: many sponsors are not effective, and the strong initial findings will continue. Parents with children in the weaker models would be discouraged, and planners would be encouraged to expand prematurely the use of the stronger models. The release of findings demands as much rational decision making as do questions of measurement, sampling, and so on.

The obligation to give data to the various constituencies demanding results from Follow Through raises another problem. Parents, teachers, and sponsors need data on individual children, and they need it as soon as testing is completed in order to make decisions about the progress of children and the short-term effectiveness of curriculum innovations. State coordinators of the Title I program of the Elementary and Secondary Education Act need the data because Follow

Through is partially supported by Title I funds, and they are required to report the impact of Title I dollars within six months after the school year is completed. Follow Through's data collection, processing, analysis, and reporting cycle is approximately fourteen months, thus satisfying no one. Even if the timing were corrected, it is doubtful whether the content of the data would be equally useful to parents, teachers, sponsors, school boards, and planners. In Follow Through the constituencies have not only been disappointed because of the timing and content of the data and begun to question the potential usefulness of the evaluation, but the issues of what instruments to use, the number of questions to be addressed, and the sampling to be done have become increasingly confusing. Any school intervention study that requires massive testing faces the question of whether to share data or to have the children tested only for its own purposes.

The reporting dates for major studies of the Follow Through cohorts fall between 1974 and 1978, emphasizing the amount of time that longitudinal studies necessarily take. The interim analyses of pupil outcomes have concentrated on differences between Follow Through and other pupils and differences among sponsors. Differences between the two groups of pupils are hard to discern because the planned variations study presumes that sponsors place different emphases on various aspects of the program. Looking for an overall difference assumes that the average emphasis in a given domain is greater within Follow Through than outside. There is no way to determine whether this is true, and the experiment was not designed to answer such a question. The questions that make the most sense are those that involve comparisons among models.

The first body of data that permit adequate model comparisons are the first-year results on the third cohort children who attended kindergarten in 1971–72. The raw and adjusted scores on the Metropolitan Achievement Test (MAT) and the Wide Range Achievement Test (WRAT) suggest that the highly structured models have the greatest effects. Table 1 indicates how many of the eleven models analyzed showed effects greater than their comparison group on the tests, and lists the sponsors for whose programs there was a positive and statistically significant difference between the treatment and comparison groups. The results are based on scores adjusted to control for some of the differences between the groups; the pattern of effects is similar for the raw and adjusted scores. Because these are short-term effects,

**Table 1. Effects in First Year of Follow Through on Children Who Entered Third Cohort Program in Kindergarten**

| | | Model group scores higher than comparison group scores | |
| --- | --- | --- | --- |
| Test | | Number of models, in total of 11 | Especially strong models[a] |
| Metropolitan Achievement Test (MAT) | | | |
| Word analysis | | 6 | Englemann-Becker Model Behavior Analysis Approach |
| Reading | | 9 | Englemann-Becker Model Behavior Analysis Approach High/Scope Model |
| Numbers | | 5 | Englemann-Becker Model Behavior Analysis Approach Individualized Early Learning Program |
| Wide Range Achievement Test (WRAT) | | 9 | Englemann-Becker Model Behavior Analysis Approach |

a. See pp. 6–9, above, for a description of the models. The only models significantly lower than their comparisons were Bank Street College of Education Approach on the MAT word analysis and numbers and the WRAT, and Tucson Early Education Model on the MAT numbers.

they should not be interpreted as a negative finding for the less structured approaches. They fit the expectation of the sponsors that those that emphasize achievement will show the greatest short-term effects on achievement. The sponsors that do not emphasize short-term accomplishments are not being adequately assessed by these data. It is nevertheless encouraging to note that in the first set of data that permit sponsor comparisons the results match the expectations.

The only noncognitive variable analyzed in the third cohort sample is attendance. It shows no difference between Follow Through and control groups and no pattern across sponsors.

Sample groups of teachers have been questioned to assess demographic characteristics, degree of the treatments' implementation, and attitudes. Only the results on attitudes have been analyzed; though difficult to interpret, they indicate that teachers are satisfied with their Follow Through models.

The design of the Follow Through study calls for parent interviews in the first year of a cohort and again when the children complete Follow Through at the end of third grade. The exiting interview is supposed to assess changes in parents and their reactions to the program. Though none of the comparisons has been completed, analyses of the entry interviews show a relatively more favorable attitude on the part of Follow Through parents toward the schools and the progress of their children after the first few months of the encounter than among parents of the control group children.

DAVID P. WEIKART

BERNARD A. BANET

# Model Design Problems
# in Follow Through

The idea of planned variation may have been totally logical at the national level, but at the sponsor level it was mystifying. The meeting in Washington of prospective sponsors to present their various orientations to curriculum, the idea that evaluation could be done by a third agency, the meeting in a hotel room to add Head Start Planned Variation, and the assumption that each sponsor had a complete package to present—all created a feeling of bewilderment and even of madness. It was a credit to everyone that something happened, a project was born, and people worked extraordinarily hard to fit the pieces into a constantly changing jigsaw puzzle.

Thousands of people eventually became deeply involved in making both the Follow Through and the Head Start Planned Variation experiment work. An examination of the important problems that arose in developing and implementing one of the models in those experiments may be helpful to the future of planned variation studies and may suggest the prospects for educational reform.

## Development of the Model

The High/Scope cognitively oriented curriculum model is intended to blend purposeful teaching with child-initiated activity.[1] It developed out of a five-year study in the use of a specially designed curriculum for preschool children. Data from the study showed that the children's

1. For a description of the model, see p. 6, above.

scores on intelligence tests increased consistently and repeatedly and that their academic achievements held up well over a long term.

The theories and methods used in the preschool education study were translated into the plan for the Follow Through model. But methods that had worked in a controlled experiment proved woefully inadequate for a field trial. Workshops in which the Piagetian developmental theory and the essential processes in acquiring and organizing knowledge in a cognitive curriculum were explained did not prepare teachers to adapt the new idea in their classrooms. Trying to graft the cognitive curriculum on the normal classroom program set up impossible conflicts in teaching styles, content orientation, and roles of classroom participants. Administrators complained that teachers were generally unable to map out whole new approaches to teaching and that they needed explicit directions and specific materials and activities. Administrators questioned the usefulness of the curriculum theory; teachers who made the commitment to the theory, on the other hand, seemed to surrender to it. Instead of developing strong, independent views of how to apply the theory, they seemed to lose their self-confidence, becoming dependent and frustrated.

To combat this problem, commercial materials that reflected the Piagetian theory were introduced into the classroom. As the teaching staffs responded, a genuinely independent program began. But in addition to a theory base and an alternative curriculum structure, new classroom methods were needed. Reorganizing the classroom and the class day is not as simple as it may sound. Teachers depend for support on administrators, parents, and other teachers; though it is less obvious, they also depend on the physical environment and daily routine. Once room arrangements were altered and the daily routine was centered on child-initiated activities, programs and classrooms that had been immune to the new curriculum began to change.

By the end of this phase in the program's evolution the model had grown from an assumption that theory could automatically be transferred to practice in the classroom to include different classroom operations and new teaching materials, and finally a restructuring of the classroom and the routine. At the end of five years of development the new curriculum seemed to be a possible educational alternative. Most of the Follow Through sponsors who follow a developmental approach are probably in the same position.

The planned variation studies represent the first major attempt to examine the clash of philosophies among educational reformers. The basic problem in moving away from the accepted technological containers for school content is the imperative to accept the new programs as a personal act of faith, because they are not an obvious extension of the traditional ways of teaching.

## Field Implementation as Teacher Training

The pressures to mount the Follow Through program in the field, with practically no lead time, meant that most of the training for teachers occurred on site. Teachers learned a model by teaching in it; they actually confronted, in the classroom, the task of applying strategies and objectives identified by the sponsor.

It was a training environment guaranteed to produce frustration and struggle, but it was also more likely than a survey or methods course in a school of education to produce real growth in teaching skills. The planned variation environments were among the first in which the classroom performance of preschool and early elementary school teachers was systematically evaluated, over time, by professional educators in terms of more or less explicit criteria provided by a model.

### Early Expectations

The revolutionary means of teacher training followed in the planned variation experiment gradually altered the assumptions that a model could be described in largely verbal terms, with perhaps a few charts and diagrams, and that this description, presented in a workshop, could persuade teachers to radically modify their teaching behavior the following year. To expect that teachers could be retrained in one magic week—even with the later constant support of a project director and curriculum assistant—was absurd.

The financial and verbal commitment of a school district to a model did not mean that everyone, least of all teachers, needed only to be told about the model in order to implement it. There were problems both of motivating teachers to change their teaching styles and of supporting orderly change in the classrooms rather than expecting the revolution to come overnight. The early workshops that were expected to stimulate teachers to create open, active classroom environments where before there had been teacher domination and reliance on highly abstract materials were well received. The new ways of doing things were enthusiastically accepted; but a few months later, change was difficult to detect in the classrooms.

### Problems in In-service Training

The gulf between workshop session and classroom implementation raised questions about the relation between teacher training activities and job performance. Apparently the teacher's repertory and the teacher's perception of the constraints imposed by the local school authorities and some parents are not amenable to lightning-fast change. Abstract theoretical principles are not easily applied after a few hours of workshop experience that is itself remote from the classroom. Training naturally turns increasingly to concrete teaching strategies that put theoretical conceptions into practice and to concrete examples provided by classroom settings, either at the center or on film or videotape.

Some high-priority issues in in-service training must be dealt with from the beginning, particularly physical arrangement of the room and the structure of the daily routine. Modifying these structures does not guarantee anything more than superficial change—for example, it is possible to teach reading in the same old way even if the teacher is working with only five children at a time instead of the whole class. But it is not possible to move toward an individualized learning setting without first modifying the physical environment and the time schedule of a classroom.

Changes that modify what teachers learn from children must also be initiated. Children can be powerful shapers of adults in a classroom. If such processes as the planning by children for themselves can begin to operate, the teacher will begin to see that children are capable of making choices and decisions and will be willing to support and extend these skills. But the teacher must first give the new process a chance.

In implementing a model, teachers can become quite paranoid. They are under constant observation and notice that a number of people have explicit but differing expectations about how they should be functioning. One way to reduce this inevitable paranoia is to talk about activities and classroom practices in terms of providing better learning experiences for children; with this focus, teachers are less likely to perceive evaluation as a subtle attack on their professional competence.

Often teachers must face the critical opposition of outsiders. Principals may want things done the old way—one suggested that a teacher "do things the way those Ypsilanti people want them done" only when the consultants were in the school. Fourth grade teachers have a knack for threatening first, second, or third grade teachers who are trying innovative methods. That "the children won't know how to deal with the traditional fourth grade" becomes a great source of anxiety.[2]

## Counterforces

Effective training in planned variation can mobilize a number of counterforces to these pressures. One is the children themselves. A classroom aglow with the excitement of active learning and a child proud of accomplishing something he has planned give the lie to criticisms that the children do not learn self-discipline or how to work independently. The mutual support within teaching teams creates a counterforce. The addition of an aide or another teacher to a classroom will provide emotional and intellectual help to a teacher learning a new method.

Another new counterforce is the curriculum assistant, who gives much closer supervision in program implementation than has ever been given before. For perhaps the first time in many schools, someone other than the teacher has been vitally concerned with the content and processes of classroom learning. The curriculum assistant is concerned not only with the smooth functioning of the physical plant and with reducing conflicts and responding to requests, but spends a significant amount of time in each classroom each week, raising curriculum questions and helping teachers plan and evaluate.

The full potential of the assistant's role is just beginning to be realized. In Head Start the inexperienced paraprofessional teachers were especially responsive to the leadership of curriculum assistants. Neither the overworked education or project directors in previous Head Start programs nor the normal public school principal can perform this service. The use of a program specialist or curriculum assistant to supervise classroom teachers deserves further study for clues as to roles and functions that simply are not performed in U.S. schools.

2. One nonmodel teacher complained that Follow Through had not taught the children self-discipline and that they were very hard to handle; but his definition of self-discipline was that children would do exactly as they were told. In another site several successful Follow Through children were failing during their fourth grade year until they learned to sit in their seats and follow directions.

The curriculum assistant, supported by field consultants and trained in workshops, was the core of the training process that evolved in the High/Scope Model. Training could be a continuing process, related to classroom experience rather than just to theory. Experience as classroom teachers was especially valuable as training for curriculum assistants. The teacher who enjoys the classroom and is effective there does not necessarily, however, become an effective supervisor of other teachers. Changing the behavior of classroom teachers without alienating them is a subtle task. It is easy to be a hostile critic or a "nice guy" who says that everything is being done just perfectly. The honest but helpful teacher trainer cannot be mass produced, but some individuals do grow in that role and some are naturally good at it.

In an open-framework program, teachers are expected to apply certain strategies to the design of educational environments and activities, and to try to understand, evaluate, and apply developmental goals to children individually. In Follow Through there was no functioning prototype for these goals and strategies. As a prototype was developed, the job of explaining what the High/Scope Model was became easier. The process of developing a model and simultaneously training others to use it put a strain on everyone. But it made clear that it was an implementation package not simply a classroom curriculum that was being developed. It also prevented the model from becoming a static derivation from theory, a set of a priori assumptions.

Ultimately each teacher must experiment in the classroom, within the framework of the model, to discover the most effective approaches for a particular group of children. Therefore, teachers may be given some useful guidance, but training is effective only when it leads to new approaches in the classroom that are initiated to meet needs that the teachers themselves perceive. This is a long-term process involving several adults as well as the children. It would be a good base for any teacher training program.

### Implementation: The Realities

The selection of a model sponsor by a community was the first major test of the political realities of planned variation. Generally speaking, the choice was based on trivial reasons. At times, however, it was made after a hard-fought election campaign. In Seattle, in debate-style presentations, a hard-line academic model and the more open High/Scope Model were explained to the board and parents responsible for selection of the sponsor. The contrast between the two models led to bitter and angry arguments among parents. Four years after the electors had made their choice, elements of the battle were still being fought.

After a model was selected, communities tried to understand the sponsor's approach. A planning committee of school officials, teachers, and parents usually visited the sponsor, looked at educational programs under way, and discussed the sponsor's educational philosophy. However, there was often little that these persons could really grasp about the model. Moreover, the concept of a long-term marriage between an independent school system and an outside sponsor was foreign to a generation raised on the one-day wonder, consulting-training approach. Even more than the concept of parent participation in local project decision making, the role of the sponsor was enigmatic to the planning committee.

Why did many of the schools agree to participate in these projects? The reasons seemed to range from a genuine desire to improve education in the community for all children, especially poor children, to a clear intent simply to obtain the funds and then ignore regulations, guidelines, sponsors, and parents. Communities with limited employment opportunities desperately needed job openings; some, in active competition with nearby communities, could chalk up an easy gain in the intercommunity balance by accepting Follow Through.

Once established, Follow Through became a focus of hostility in many communities. Basically the minority groups are right: there is a vast reservoir of anger and hostility toward low-income people, particularly those who are members of minority groups. Follow Through and Head Start, as programs for such groups, attracted major opposition simply because "they get too much already." One community was upset because of the dental treatment program for the youngsters, another angered because of the free lunch provided to poor children. Attempts were made to divert Follow Through dollars to other community needs; requirements that Follow Through funds actually be used as the federal program intended were resented and resisted.

As programs became established, hostility toward the participants (more common in small southern and western communities than in the problem-plagued large cities) often became intense as the Follow Through parents began to be more active politically. One board commented that "the parents can ask but they had better not try to tell us anything." A superintendent said that Follow Through was a squeaky wheel on the wagon. "Now, there is no point," he said, "to a squeaky wheel. We'll just take it off the wagon." Ultimately, politically active parents became recognized forces in their communities. Indeed, in the spring of 1973 one Follow Through site, when the board refused to meet its request for continuation of the project, initiated a recall election to replace the board members with their own community representatives.

### Constraints on Model Implementation

Pressure—from state legislators, school boards, and even commercial publishing houses—for educational "accountability" has become a major force acting on Follow Through. Basically, the idea is sound: establish realistic goals for education, and then hold teachers and ultimately children accountable for reaching those goals. California has molded this concept into law; Colorado and Michigan have moved rapidly toward a system of statewide minimally acceptable objectives for each grade level.

An opposing trend, toward open education, has also been gathering support. The accountability trend, however, poses a serious threat to the integrity of the open planned variation models. Basically, accountability is appealing because it uses technocratic solutions to educational problems—if children are to learn to read, direct teaching of reading is certainly the most effective way to accomplish that end. What could be simpler than to have the state pick up this theme and hold sponsors in the state responsible for reaching these goals? However, the objectives against which programs and teachers are usually held accountable best match those of models that follow "teacher-proof" curricula. This leaves the majority of Follow Through sponsors—those with means and ends other than the direct teaching of academic skills—in a quandary. Surprisingly, many parents and educational officials are unaware of fundamental differences among models. In one community an open-framework model was accused of failure after programmed-instruction models had failed to show positive results. In general, local communities see models only within the context of local concerns. The parents of children in Follow Through programs are usually preoccupied with political survival of the program; to the dismay of sponsors, they seldom have time for or interest in discussing, say, the relative merits of a Piagetian and a Skinnerian solution to an educational problem.

The goals of planned variation models, especially in Head Start, have also clashed with those of federal regional offices and of local school systems. Local school districts' concern with academic degrees, tenure, and administration has often placed difficult demands on Head Start centers. Setting aside time for home visits and for staff planning in the official school day has raised critical problems and local districts have attempted to impose their choice of classroom materials. Programs run by community action agencies tend to be less bound by public school traditionalism, but they do not escape pressures from the school, especially if they are dependent on the school for classroom space, cafeteria services, or transportation. Conflict between community action and the local schools weakened and eventually eliminated a strong program in one planned variation site where community action goals relating to community organization took precedence over the Heart Start program.

### The Brighter Side

In the Head Start Planned Variation study one bright spot has been the general consultant. When it was announced that neutral consultants would observe their work, model sponsors were deeply concerned—and more so when they found the consultants' budget frequently exceeded their own. However, the consultants proved to be remarkably able to intervene neutrally or supportively, no matter what the viewpoint represented by the model. They made a major contribution in the Head Start program.

The consultants' role has been more ambiguous in Follow Through, for their theoretical biases often show through. One consultant, feeling that a reading program was not effective, set up a review session with the teachers to introduce alternatives; another left flyers about a commercial reading program. One, believing the model's focus was not sufficiently behavioral, introduced training sessions for the staff on the preparation of behavioral objectives.

Many general consultants have, however, saved programs from certain death by timely and professional intervention. Many have added greatly to sponsors' understanding of the teacher's learning process. But general consultants have also contributed to the feeling that at times the sponsor is being corralled.

None of the other forces operating on Follow Through models can compare with that the participants in the project exerted. Their pressure is sufficiently unique in its effect to warrant major attention as a way of shaping effective education. Ordinarily, an educational experiment is put into operation at one site on the initiative of a group of outsiders and for their own purposes. Seldom is reform in education accomplished by outsiders; but reform is almost never accomplished by local people alone (a fact that is rarely conceded). It is essential that a process of interaction be established for effective change.

Neither Follow Through nor Head Start Planned Variation operates on a one-site, one-shot philosophy. Funding for the participants is long term; Follow Through in half a decade of consistent developmental work under demanding circumstances has produced change. And the program offers the sponsor an opportunity to work at many sites instead of only one.

The most important advantage is the fact that Follow Through arrangements with communities are almost in the form of marriages that cannot be annulled. This forced togetherness over five years has provided ample time to see issues come and go, to isolate the central problems, and to develop programs and services.

### The Value of Comparing Models

The logic of the planned variation approach—the basic logic of scientific verification—is compelling. Some departures from true experimental procedures must be made in the interest of assuring the relevance of the findings, but the basic idea is to relate the models (as predictor variables) to outcomes—usually child outcomes. Can the planned variation methodology be expected to yield useful data? Or are the researchers and policymakers doomed to findings of "no differences" among educational methods?

The experiments so far have not turned up significant differences among treatment groups. Yet it is not necessarily the methodology that is at fault even in "quasi-experiments" like Follow Through and Head Start Planned Variation. What is needed may be a clearer conceptualization of models, outcomes, and intervening processes, as well as better educational treatments for the researcher to evaluate.

Each model in a systematic variation should be explicit enough to provide fairly readily describable results of specific aspects of the treatment. If this strategy is to pay off, the models must actually be implemented, producing some evidence of having systematic effects on classrooms in the field situations. The standards used to measure outcomes must reflect the central concerns of the policymaker or of the model sponsors and they must be designed to expose unintended effects.

These criteria have not been fully met in Follow Through. Models thought to have been replicable have dissolved into unreality. The gap between conception and reality may be the result of inadequate conceptualization and specification of the model. This is especially likely if the model developer is asked to implement a model in the field before a local prototype is in operation. A model may change so much over time that its character is elusive. Or all of the models in a program may systematically converge under uniform pressures from the field. The training and monitoring systems may be so inadequate that the model cannot operate properly. Or the classroom personnel and others responsible for implementing the model may actively resist it.

The reliability of the treatment variable has been diluted in all of these ways throughout the history of planned variation experiments. Increasingly, however, sophisticated data are being gathered on the ways that models are actually implemented in a planned variation experiment. In the future the relationship between a sponsor's prototype and the field models will be more easily gauged.

There may be important differences in the extent to which various models can be specified and implemented. A programmed model, aimed at removing variations between teachers, may be ready for evaluation long before an open-framework or child-centered model is. The latter do not automatically homogenize teachers' behavior by providing materials for children, equipment, or a script for the teachers. Open-framework and child-centered models may have some long-run advantages, but they are treatments that are not easily implemented. A planned variation experiment that stresses initial results may miss this important fact. Follow Through fortunately is permitting adequate time for developing prototypes, delivery systems, and implementation. Head Start Planned Variation may reflect the comparatively mature state of the program before its implementation.

Outcome measures are even more of a problem than definition of treatment variables. The measures used are those that are available— IQ tests and standard achievement tests. It would be foolish to abandon the planned variation experiments because no differences show up on IQ scores or in performances of Piagetian tasks. These measures are designed to reflect achievement according to age rather than years of formal instruction. Where differences do appear in these measures, it is usually a sign that a powerful method is at work; failure to differentiate models by these measures should not be cause for despair.

Reliance on standard achievement tests also works against gathering a wide range of information from a planned variation experiment. Many models would not normally aim at raising achievement test scores in the earliest years, so why judge them on these criteria alone? Other measurements should develop naturally out of the objectives specified by the innovative models. The High/Scope Foundation, for example, is working on measures of productive communication skills to supplant conventional reading achievement tests.

To date, planned variation results do not seem to have helped to identify superior and inferior ways of accomplishing important long-run educational objectives. Specific outcomes seem simply to result from the degree to which a model emphasizes behavior related to the criterion measures. Empirically as well as logically the less teachable the criterion tasks and the more universal the criterion-related behaviors, the less likely is the planned variation technique to yield differences.

Just as important as skill outcomes are affective outcomes—intended and unintended. Are children doing well on reading achievement tests but learning to hate reading and fear school? It may be as necessary to examine the quality of the environments as it is to measure immediate outcomes.

Planned variation experiments may prove most useful as prods to curriculum development, the refinement of evaluation techniques, and the generation of new hypotheses about changing individuals and institutions. Rather than producing conclusive validation methods, they may have the heuristic value of the nonconclusive experiment that is obvious in other sciences. The possibility of their serving as a stimulus to further work is more evident now than it was at the beginning of the planned variation efforts. Further experiments should take this into account; the feedback process should be explicitly built into planned variation and given greater emphasis than the summative evaluations. Already, mountains of narrative accounts as well as quantitative data have been collected. Model sponsors for the most part have not benefited from these reports. A less rigid conception of planned variation research might have led to feedback of data to the sponsors as they were developing delivery systems.

## Implications for Planned Variation Research

After five years of experience in planned variation experiments both on the national scale and in a small-scale project it is apparent that some phases in the research dissemination cycle should not be tampered with (see Figure 1).[3] The cycle begins with a tightly controlled research project and moves through the development of training materials, to demonstration and field testing, and finally to the dissemination phase. The first stage in the cycle must be a tightly controlled study, adhering closely to true experimental design. The objectives should be simple and clearly stated and should be randomly assigned to treatment and control groups; procedures should be carefully documented; and evaluation should focus on nonquantitative information about the experiment itself, and on outcomes of the program only if instruments exist for assessing them effectively. The purpose of the program should be viewed as frankly experimental, and the specific outcomes of the work truly unknown.

The next stage is for developing training materials and methods. To meet the needs identified in the experimental study, film, videotape, manuals, handbooks, reading lists, and practical systems for gaining experience rapidly may be required. They will be used principally in the third phase to instruct trainees in the program criteria. Development of training materials will continue throughout the experiment to meet the needs of different staff and situations, as will development of instruments for measuring outcomes.

3. Between 1968 and 1970 the High/Scope Foundation conducted a tightly controlled study of three models of preschool education. There were, on the whole, no initial or subsequent differences among the models on intellectual and achievement tests; children in all three models did very well on both. Direct teaching of academic skills in the programmed model offered none of the supposed advantages over the other methods, and the traditionally child-centered model did not exhibit the widely reported inability to produce effective results. It appears that specific curricula may have less impact on the general success or failure of models than do the demands and expectations that surround the operation of a complex project.

**Figure 1. High/Scope Research and Dissemination Procedure: Stages in the Development of an Intervention Project**[a]

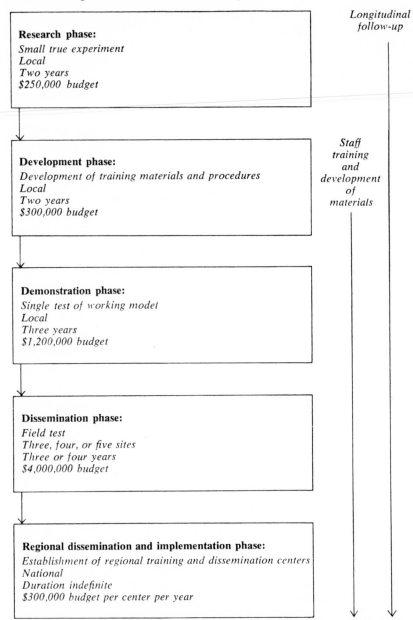

a. The number of years and the budget amounts for each phase are rough estimates. Budget figures do not include the costs of developing instruments to measure results, follow-up studies, staff training, or the development of new materials.

In the third phase, the developed educational program is demonstrated in a setting that approximates a regular field operation. The characteristics of the operating personnel are keyed to those of the people who are expected to operate the project in the field. For example, paraprofessionals are used if that is intended in the final phase. In this phase the essential components for effective field operations are developed: the curriculum, the system to deliver it, the training procedures necessary to the program's implementation, the staff model to be used, and quality control methods to assure successful field implementation. Within the framework of the original research project, adaptations and improvements are made to build on experience and to meet practical political and other demands. However, the central focus of the project is retained; the basic design is not changed. In this the most critical phase, retaining the intent of the original project is very difficult. The special objectives are to test the training systems, to further develop measurement instruments, and to replicate the design established in the first phase. Evaluation is focused on the program's form in order to develop quality control measures and to link specific procedures with desired outcomes.

Next is a limited field test under natural circumstances. The number of sites is held down so that effective control will not be lost. The training methods and materials are ready for field use; the components essential to implementation are ready. Research revolves around large policy issues, such as the potential impact on populations to be served. The quality control procedures are primarily designed to produce monitoring information, and indicate comparability with the original study and demonstration project. The original sponsor usually remains active in this stage.

Finally, the education program is ready for dissemination to many sites. The curriculum, training program, delivery system, staff model, and quality control procedures are clearly known and available. Research on the effect on differing populations and under differing circumstances may continue, but the basic program is well documented and capable of achieving the intended results. Both sponsorship and the number of programs are broadened at this stage.

The five stages represent a twelve-year sequence—not a means of providing information quickly for policy decisions—whose goal is the effective delivery of an educational program with the ability to obtain consistently the desired results.

In Follow Through, because of the pressure for policy information, most sponsors bypassed the early phases and went immediately into the field-test phase. Hence many of the dilemmas in interpreting data from the planned variation experiments. In future studies it is essential that adequate time and resources be devoted to preparation. The more complex the proposed ideas and the more they diverge from current practice, the greater is the need for preparation.

If true alternatives to current educational practices are to be developed, experiments must be carried on in a dynamic system. The developer must allow for and respond to pressure from the participants —teacher, parents, administrators, and the children themselves. Educational programs must be a synthesis of theory and practice and must continually be reshaped by developers and participants alike if they are to remain effective. Once the developer is committed to a dynamic system, he must have enough time to produce the changes he desires.

Attention should focus on creating major changes in education. Programs with what are really minor differences in methods of teaching phonics to first graders have never produced significant differences. Why should they in Follow Through? Whole new educational systems with broadly differentiated goals and outcome effects are needed. The grafting of various program parts—of teachers with the traditional training, school structures with standardized space and equipment, fairly uniform calendars (five hours a day, nine hundred hours a year) is not the best way to produce radically new approaches. New systems must evolve that represent dramatically different ways of approaching and supporting child development. Why teach reading as such at all? Where does the responsibility lie for a child's learning, and how soon and in what way does the child become able to assume this responsibility? The situation-induced training and experience that planned variation provides is unique in education. Follow Through is just the beginning of an extended process of development, not a completed demonstration of what exists. New planned variation experiments must accept this difference.

From the beginning of the planned variation experiments, much of the problem appeared to be in training teachers. Altering teaching behavior has proved to be extraordinarily difficult. To an important extent a teacher's behavior is shaped by the expectations of parents, peers, administrators, and, indeed, the children themselves. There is no such thing as a "trained teacher"; training must be continuous. A training system must begin at the teacher's point of need and gradually shift as the teacher gains sophistication in the methodology.

There is a pressing need to develop new assessment strategies. The evaluation of competence in school now has little relation to the long-term objectives most parents and educators really hold for children. Reading is not marking the appropriate box on the multiple-choice test; most Americans don't read regularly. Mathematics is not the multiplication table; whole segments of society fear numbers and numerical operations. New evaluation tools are needed that tap the broader social goals of education. The direction seems to be toward radically different measurement objectives (for example, using writing as a test of reading), and toward recognizing that the value of a curriculum cannot be measured unless the degree of its implementation is known. A program must be captured in process through observations and testing, in the conditions under which children are functioning. And longitudinal effects must be considered. Children in Ypsilanti who had participated in a preschool project ten years before, for example, were placed less frequently in special education classes than children from the control group. Longitudinal follow-up is critical for assessing the optimal ages for learning specific skills and for uncovering unexpected effects in areas not directly related to treatment.

Planned variation experiments are potentially a solid method for developing alternative educational procedures. The statistical data produced in the first round may be unclear, but that is the fault of the sponsors' concepts. Planned variation has produced a base for more effective future experiments and for effective educational alternatives.

LOIS-ELLIN DATTA

# Design of the Head Start
# Planned Variation
# Experiment

Since 1968, the planned variation design has become
a popular form of social policy research—perhaps too popular, since
its practical drawbacks have been largely unknown, and the characteristics of the design itself but little examined. The unusually extensive analyses in the Head Start Planned Variation (HSPV) study increasingly
are showing what is and what is not negotiable in design, in measurement, and at various stages of program development if strong inferences about the relative effects of different treatments are to be drawn.

The contributions that Head Start Planned Variation has made to educational research and to the clarification of issues in early childhood programming seem substantial and possibly worth the nearly $7 million
invested in the program. However, those who anticipated that the study,
although imperfect, would be a valuable source of information in formu-
lating policy on early intervention are less likely to be satisfied than are
researchers who saw the limitations of the study from its beginning.[1]

Both political necessity (that is, policymaking, legislative, organiza-

1. For an optimistic view, see Joseph S. Wholey and others, *Federal Evalua-
tion Policy: Analyzing the Effects of Public Programs* (Washington: Urban Insti-
tute, 1970); and Alice M. Rivlin, *Systematic Thinking for Social Action* (Brook-
ings Institution, 1971). In contrast, see David K. Cohen, "Politics and Research:
The Evaluation of Social Action Programs in Education," *Review of Educational
Research,* vol. 40 (April 1970), pp. 213–38; and P. Michael Timpane, "Educational
Experimentation in National Social Policy," *Harvard Educational Review,* vol. 40
(November 1970), pp. 547–66.

tional, and managerial factors) and limitations in the state of the art of design, measurement, analysis, and educational theory have influenced the Planned Variation study. On balance, political necessity more than the state of the art has determined its characteristics. The conditions under which planned variation would be a desirable strategy are demanding. Social researchers might well consider these limitations in comparison with those of other experimental strategies that require a less remarkable conjunction of favorable circumstances.

Within the federal establishment the principal influences on Head Start Planned Variation came from policy managers and analysts, typified by personnel in the Bureau of the Budget (more recently the Office of Management and Budget), program managers at various levels within Head Start, and research administrators. The objectives of these three sets of actors sometimes conflict. Budget Bureau personnel are responsible for ensuring that moneys are spent as the administration and Congress intend and that programs are well managed. The bureau, inclined to rely on economic and administrative evidence to sort out the claims of competing programs, had become increasingly critical of the War on Poverty programs in the late 1960s, and it urged Head Start to become more experimental in seeking effective ways to help children.

Head Start program managers, like other program managers, concentrate on the delivery of services. Warmly human people, touched by the plight of children in poverty, they tend to be advocates rather than critics and to seek expansion of their programs. Frequently they are fascinated with new ideas and are aware of room for improvement, but must live with some program of deficiencies beyond their control. Improvement, continuity, and delivery of services rather than testing basic program assumptions usually have the highest priority for program managers.

Research administrators are interested in realizing their vision of good research; they view studies whose design, measurement, and data analysis will "tell it like it is" as the best long-run research strategy for improving the quality of life. Often impatient with the demands that program managers must balance and dissatisfied with the short research turnaround needed by policymakers, research administrators may be reluctant to cut and fit design ideals to the needs of the real world.

Despite the shared goals and the compassion and integrity of each of the three parties, some conflict over strategy in policy research is probably inevitable.

## Description of the Study

Since June 1969, Head Start Planned Variation has been an experimental program to determine which of several early childhood curricula have the greatest immediate effect on Head Start children. It has also sought information on whether participation in well-planned, well-implemented, continuous programs in the preschool and early primary years would yield continuous development in the children. Usually, preschool interventions are found to have an immediate favorable impact; without further interventions after entry into school, however, the control group catches up, and the scores of both experimental and control groups gradually decline after the third grade.[2]

Also, by 1969, it was clear from studies of children participating in Head Start and other preschool programs that their gains on a variety of measures varied in statistical and educational significance from marginal to quite substantial.[3] While establishing the immediate benefits of Head Start, the studies gave few indications of what programs yield the greatest immediate effects, in what areas of development, and for which children. Is there one best program for most children in most areas? Are many approaches equally effective? Do programs have specific, rather than general, effects? Or is the most variance accounted for by interactions among the program, area, child, and family characteristics—an hypothesis popular among childhood educators?

2. See Lois-ellin Datta, "A Report on Evaluation Studies of Project Head Start" (paper presented at the American Psychological Association convention, September 1969; processed); Marian S. Stearns, *Report on Preschool Programs: The Effects of Preschool Programs on Disadvantaged Children and Their Families* (U.S. Department of Health, Education, and Welfare, Office of Child Development, 1971); Sheldon H. White and others, *Federal Programs for Young Children: Review and Recommendations,* 4 vols. (U.S. Government Printing Office, 1973); Frances D. Horowitz and Lucile Y. Paden, "The Effectiveness of Environmental Intervention Programs," in Bettye M. Caldwell and Henry N. Ricciuti (eds.), *Review of Child Development Research,* vol. 3, *Child ꞌDevelopment and Social Policy* (University of Chicago Press, 1973); Urie Bronfenbrenner, *A Report on Longitudinal Evaluations of Preschool Programs,* vol. 2, *Is Early Intervention Effective?* DHEW Publication (OHD) 74-25 (U.S. Department of Health, Education, and Welfare, 1974); and Harvey A. Averch and others, *How Effective is Schooling? A Critical Review and Synthesis of Research Findings* (Santa Monica, Calif.: Rand Corp., 1972).

3. See Averch and others, *How Effective Is Schooling?* and Stearns, *Report on Preschool Programs,* for discussions of initial status, absolute gain, and final level achieved in terms of statistical and educational significance.

The studies also left unresolved the question of the long-term effects of different early childhood education programs. One- or two-year center-based preschool programs for disadvantaged children have not yet been able to show substantial, lasting effects after the third or fourth grade.[4] Many longitudinal studies report that some effects on children, parents, and institutions hold up, but among studies there is little consistency in the findings; and even the statistically reliable differences tend to be small.[5] Sometimes subgroups for whom the preschool effects are evident long after the child has entered regular school can be identified, but again the samples are small and the findings are not repeated across studies.[6] In sum, it has not been proven that one- or two-year center-based preschool programs can *by themselves* help children from low-income families or children with developmental lags succeed in regular public schools when success is defined by cognitive, academic, or social-adjustment criteria.[7]

4. See Bronfenbrenner, *Is Early Intervention Effective?* Weikart, however, reports that, as late as the end of the eighth grade, children from control groups are more likely than children who participated in his preschool experiment to be in special education classes or in grades below those expected for their age levels. Personal communication from David P. Weikart, 1972; and Weikart and others, *Longitudinal Results of the Ypsilanti Perry Preschool Project,* Project 2494, Grant OE 4-10-085 (Ypsilanti, Mich.: High/Scope Educational Research Foundation, August 1970), p. 65, Table 4-1.

5. Sally Ryan (ed.), *A Report on Longitudinal Evaluations of Preschool Programs,* vol. 1: *Longitudinal Evaluations,* DHEW Publication (OHD) 74-24 (U.S. Department of Health, Education, and Welfare, 1974).

6. Interactive studies include Ryan (ed.), *Longitudinal Evaluations;* Weikart, *Longitudinal Results of the Ypsilanti Perry Preschool Project;* Joan S. Bissell, "The Cognitive Effects of Preschool Programs for Disadvantaged Children" (doctoral dissertation, Harvard University, 1970); and E. Kuno Beller, "Impact of Early Education on Disadvantaged Children," in Ryan (ed.), *Longitudinal Evaluations,* pp. 15–48. As an example of the complexity of this literature, Bissell found no sex interaction with immediate IQ gains; Beller and Weikart both report that the effects of early education are more durable in girls than in boys. Louise B. Miller and others, *Experimental Variation of Head Start Curricula: A Comparison of Current Approaches* (University of Louisville, Department of Psychology, progress reports 1–10, 1970–73); and Edsel L. Erickson and others, *Experiments in Head Start and Early Education: The Effects of Teacher Attitude and Curriculum Structure on Preschool Disadvantaged Children* (Western Michigan University, 1969), report that boys suffer most from non-participation in compensatory preschool and primary school programs. In an extensive interactive analysis, Elizabeth Herzog, Carol H. Newcomb, and Ira H. Cisin, "Double Deprivation: The Less They Have, The Less They Learn," in Ryan (ed.), *Longitudinal Evaluations,* chap. 5, found similar effects on grade placement outcomes but complex interactions when initial IQ is simultaneously considered.

7. When research evidence is viewed stringently, there is little basis for en-

The catch-up phenomenon—the increase in IQ or achievement scores of children in the first grade who have had no preschool experience— is variously interpreted as showing that the cognitive processes are little affected by environment or that human development is continuous and requires comprehensive, early, and continuous support.[8] Head Start Planned Variation, in cooperation with Follow Through, was intended to test the continuity hypothesis, to ask the questions: Would continuity of experience from preschool through early primary school in a well-planned, well-implemented, comprehensive program have sustained and substantial effects? Would preschools add little or much to the effects of a good primary experience?

The study was aimed at improving Head Start by incorporating effective curricula into the daily program, and at justifying preschool intervention by demonstrating the magnitude and durability of its benefits when preschool was followed by enriched, comprehensive, and educationally continuous primary schooling. The immediate and longer-term effects of twelve preschool models were to be compared on the basis of the participating children's cognitive, scholastic, and motivational development. Three waves of Head Start children (in 1969, 1970, and 1971) were involved—some two thousand children each year. About one-third of the children attended regular Head Start classes, and the other two-thirds attended classes supervised by one of the twelve curriculum sponsors. About half of the experimental group continued in the Follow Through program under the same sponsors who had super-

thusiasm about the durability and magnitude of short-term, classroom-based compensatory or preventive programs at any age. See, for example, Averch and others, *How Effective is Schooling?;* David G. Hawkridge, Albert B. Chalupsky, and A. Oscar H. Roberts, *A Study of Selected Exemplary Programs for the Education of Disadvantaged Children* (American Institutes for Research in the Behavioral Sciences, 1968). For an even-handed review of expectations, data, and the policy implications of different interpretations of these and other data, see Godfrey Hodgson, "Do Schools Make a Difference?" *Atlantic Monthly,* March 1973.

8. Among the interpretations: a change of environment whether in preschool or in first grade will induce a spurt in the child's development; teachers teach to the neediest children and fail to build on the preschooled child's experience; children teach each other and so the Head Start children improve the performance of their non-preschooled classmates; cognition is less influenced by environment than are other characteristics, such as motivation, and thus the gains possible from a brief preschool intervention are small and nondurable; human development is a continuous process, requiring continuous environmental support; cognitive development is discontinuous and reflects the unfolding of innate perceptual-linguistic abilities, so that early intervention is unnecessary if children later are given environmental incentives to perform according to their abilities.

vised the Head Start Planned Variation models. The rest entered regular public schools.[9]

The assignment of measures to children and classes differed from year to year, and within years. Teacher assessments of child development before and after the program were collected for all children. In addition, one thousand children yearly were tested individually on measures intended to assess cognitive, scholastic, and motivational development;[10] samples of mother-child interactions and parent attitudes were also collected on this group.[11] In addition, the effectiveness of the implementation of the curriculum models was assessed in all classes by sponsor and Head Start director ratings and by teacher and teacher aide questionnaires, and in some classes through special observation by trained paraprofessionals and educational consultants.

The University of Maryland began case studies in 1969 of a small sample of randomly selected children attending sponsored and comparison classes in each of the twelve approaches; they were designed to enrich understanding of child development and curriculum effects, particularly of children's personal and social development, areas for which measurement seemed weakest.[12] In the last operational year of the program (1972), nine sponsors took advantage of the opportunity to collect and analyze data reflecting their experiences in HSPV. Head Start also

9. See Jenny Klein and Laura L. Dittman, "Head Start Planned Variation Study" (HEW, Office of Child Development, 1972; processed).

10. At the first meetings of the Head Start staff, sponsors and evaluation personnel, many sponsors showed more concern about development of the child's self-concept and sense of worth, and of the child's ability to use adult resources, to think and reason and to solve problems of daily life than about prescholastic achievement or general cognitive ability. Accordingly, great effort was made to use the best available measures of these outcomes. But due to the state of the art of measurement, adequately assessing personal and social development appeared almost impossible for the first year and possibly for several years, even with combined Head Start and Follow Through support for development of measures.

11. See Stanford Research Institute, *Implementation of Planned Variation in Head Start: Preliminary Evaluations of Planned Variation in Head Start According to Follow Through Approaches (1969–1970)*, DHEW Publication (OCD) 72-7 (HEW, Office of Child Development, 1971); Marshall S. Smith, *Some Short Term Effects of Project Head Start: A Report on the Second Year of Planned Variation— 1970–71* (Huron Institute, 1973).

12. See Laura L. Dittmann and others, *Study of Selected Children in Head Start Planned Variation, 1969–70* (HEW, Office of Child Development, 1971); Garry McDaniels and others, *Case Studies of Children in Head Start Planned Variation, 1970–1971* (HEW, Office of Child Development, 1972); David Kyle and others, *Case Studies of Children in Head Start Planned Variation, 1971–1972* (University of Maryland, Institute for Child Study, 1973).

supported some experimental tests of the effectiveness of different media in disseminating information about HSPV to parents and others. Finally, curriculum modification meant further costs for all HSPV models. Cost studies were conducted to find out how this money was spent in modifying the models—on personnel, materials, training, renovations—so that local communities could better project what it would cost to adopt a particular approach in their circumstances.

## Is HSPV a Planned Variation Experiment?

Planned variation has been defined as "sets of experimental demonstration projects, each set developed according to a single overall research design. . . . The evaluator exercises considerably more control of inputs and processes than in on-going programs and much less of the experimental design is sacrificed to operational considerations. . . . Characteristics to be varied should be those that (a) are thought to be basic variables affecting program output and (b) are structural features of program organization."[13]

In a loose sense, the term *planned variation* could describe any field experiment where the researcher has control over program characteristics. Head Start Planned Variation, since it compares the relative effects of twelve treatments indirectly under control through researcher selection of curricula to be tested, fits that prescription. There is, however, the second requirement of varying program characteristics considered to be basic to the program's purpose.

The characteristics that are "basic to program output" in an early childhood education program were uncertain in 1969, and they remain so. Until recently, studies of classroom and teacher characteristics have yielded inconsistent and weak predictions of these factors' effect on the cognitive, linguistic, achievement, and personal and social development of children. In studies up to 1974, the relation between structured programs with directed teaching and gains on cognitive and achievement measures has been more reliable than other relationships.[14]

---

13. Wholey and others, *Federal Evaluation Policy,* pp. 100, 101.
14. See Lois-ellin Datta, Carol R. McHale, and Sandra Mitchell, *The Effects of the Head Start Class Room Experience on Some Aspects of Child Development; A Summary Report of National Evaluations, 1966–1969* (HEW, Office of Child Development, 1974); Bissell, "The Cognitive Effects of Preschool Programs"; and Smith, *Some Short Term Effects.* Decker Walker and Jon Schaffarzick, "Comparing Curricula," *Review of Educational Research,* vol. 44 (Winter 1974), p. 108, conclude: "We begin as people always begin, naively, to look for

Of equal consequence for research design has been a lack of knowledge of how the structure or functions of different preschool curricula differ on variables that are thought to be of basic importance. Few reports were available in 1969 about how one program differed from another in practice, though such descriptions as "child centered" and "teacher oriented," "structured" and "unstructured," had long been applied to preschool curricula.

Neither Follow Through nor HSPV compared programs known to differ on process variables that are basic to output. Indeed, the ability to define the fundamentally important processes and to measure each curriculum in terms of the definition was so primitive that designing a true planned variation study would not have been possible.

Thus Head Start Planned Variation seems to be a comparative curriculum study rather than a rigorous planned variation project. It fails also to qualify as an experiment according to Riecken's definition:

By *experiment* is meant that one or more *treatments* (programs) are administered to some set of persons (or other units) drawn *at random* from a specified population; and that observations (or *measurements*) are made to learn how (or how much) some relevant aspect of their behavior following treatment differs from like behavior on the part of an untreated or control group also drawn at random from the same population.[15]

In HSPV, until 1971, treatments were not randomly assigned to sites, classes, or children, and there were no untreated or control groups. Site and child characteristics were confounded with sponsor characteristics; for example, the structured, academically oriented programs were in the North, parent-education sites in the South. Entry-level performance on outcome measures, as well as age and ethnicity, covaried with sponsors.

### What Did HSPV Show?

Findings from the second year analysis show that, on average, HSPV children learned at twice their usual growth rate during the program.

---

signs of superiority of innovative curricula over traditional curricula. What we found was not superiority, but parity: each curriculum did better on the distinctive parts of its own program, and each did about equally well on the parts they held in common." New data from the Follow Through classroom observation studies may justify modification of this conclusion, however.

15. Henry W. Riecken and Robert F. Boruch (eds.), *Social Experimentation: A Method for Planning and Evaluating Social Intervention* (Academic Press, 1974).

Performance differences among HSPV children of different ages increased during the program by one-half to three times. This implies that Head Start stimulated substantial acceleration in growth rates in cognitive, linguistic, and perceptual-motor domains. But overall, these growth rates were not reliably greater than those of children in unsponsored Head Start classes, implying that regular Head Start programs are as good as sponsored programs.

Finally, with a few exceptions, differences in gains were not consistently associated with individual sponsors. The observed sponsor differences indicate some specific effects for one or another curriculum, but none of the curricula was distinguished by enough specific effects to stand out as the best approach.

If these findings were accepted without reservation, their implication for policy would be that preschool intervention offered at Head Start centers is of substantial immediate benefit to the children. The immediate outcome of a treatment, however, is narrowly, rather than broadly, related to the methods used. Within a wide variety, one curriculum is as good as (or as poor as) another. Programs might safely offer a broad choice of approaches without fear of impairing child growth by withholding the best approach.

Unfortunately, HSPV provides no clear affirmation that these findings regarding sponsors reliably and accurately represent the immediate effects of the twelve programs on children and parents. Shortcomings in design, implementation, measurement, and analysis prevent this. Much has been learned about the implementation of models and the documentation of experimental practice; and important evidence of specific benefits has been developed through an elegant and ingenious series of statistical analyses. However, these analyses have not identified beyond reasonable doubt either the characteristics or the effects of the several curricula.

That the results are not those of a true experiment is due to both political circumstances and the state of the art of early childhood research. Planned variation, as a new design for federal evaluations, and the need for a comparative curriculum study linking preschool and primary school programs were both in the wind in 1968. Many of the decisions regarding the scope and timing of the Head Start Planned Variation study, the design itself, the selection of sites and contractors, and national data collection requirements reflect Head Start's responsiveness to the concern of the Bureau of the Budget and the Office of Economic Opportunity that Head Start (like many of the Johnson administration's Great Society programs) become more "experimental," that it "try out and evaluate the best of the new approaches" and demonstrate effectiveness, rather than just deliver its services.

One of the influences on HSPV was Follow Through. Follow Through sprang from a concern that the comprehensive services offered by Head Start be continued into the early primary years, since early reports suggested that the benefits of the Head Start intercession were not sustained in public school. Intended in 1967 as a service program, Follow Through because of lack of funds developed in 1968 into a large planned variation project.

The Budget Bureau's enthusiasm for the planned variation design in Follow Through was a factor in moving Head Start to a more experimental stance both in its own programs and in its relationship to Follow Through. In addition, the combination of an experimental Follow Through curriculum model that also served Head Start children in some sites was attractive to the Head Start leadership as part of their demonstration efforts. Head Start was developing such a program at full speed by January 1969.

Evaluation studies of Head Start had been carried out since 1966. Initially, in order to identify successful project approaches, extensive tests given before and after the program at sites selected on an informal basis were coupled with classroom observations and other ways of assessing program characteristics. These studies included observations of teachers and classrooms, new outcome measures, parent interviews, and analyses of the interaction among classroom characteristics, child characteristics, and other variables. Moreover, many of Head Start's fourteen research and evaluation centers had begun work on experimental designs and were urging a more systematic curriculum selection process. By the spring of 1969 the Head Start evaluation program had developed some of the research components for a planned variation study.

Comparative studies of preschool curricula were much in vogue in the late 1960s, and several planned variation studies were under way outside Head Start.[16] Yet neither singly nor collectively did they provide suf-

16. See, for example, Weikart and others, *Longitudinal Results of the Ypsilanti Perry Preschool Project;* Miller and Dyer, *Experimental Variation of Head Start Curricula;* Louis T. Di Lorenzo and others, *Prekindergarten Programs for Educationally Disadvantaged Children* (U.S. Office of Education, 1969); Merle B. Karnes, James A. Teska, and A. S. Hodgins, "The Effects of Four Programs of Class-

ficient information for national policy purposes. Head Start needed a study that would, for example, (1) test curricula in sites where they were not under the immediate control of their developers; (2) assess curriculum implementation; (3) test curricula on representative populations in representative sets of sites; (4) analyze the interaction between program effects and ethnic and socioeconomic characteristics of children; and (5) measure postexperimental effects in ordinary school settings.

Finally, in 1969, one particular study, the Westinghouse-Ohio study of Head Start,[17] resulted in a further push toward planned variations. Designed by the Office of Economic Opportunity's Research, Program Planning, and Evaluation Section as a summative assessment of Head Start as a national program, this study compared children who did and did not participate in the 1965, 1966, and 1967 summer and the 1966 and 1967 full-year Head Start programs on the bases of standardized achievement tests and of several measures of scholastic motivation and personal-social development. It also included parent interviews. The children were in the first, second, and third grades at time of testing (in the fall of 1968) and thus had attended the earliest Head Start programs. No information on pre-Head Start development, on the immediate effects of the programs, on Head Start teacher and program characteristics, or on regular school experiences was collected.

The Westinghouse-Ohio study found no differences on any measure at any grade between summer participants and nonparticipants. Differences favoring Head Start participants were found for children attending the full-year program who were tested in the first grade, with substantial differences for children who had just completed Head Start. Black, inner-city, and southern children were also likely to have higher scores on the achievement tests than their controls. No effects were found after the first grade.

The report was interpreted widely as evidence that the Head Start program was a failure, and the idea of early comprehensive intervention was found guilty by association in many quarters.

After the findings in the Westinghouse report became known, the

room Intervention on the Intellectual and Language Development of 4-Year-Old Disadvantaged Children," *American Journal of Orthopsychiatry,* vol. 40 (January 1970), pp. 58–76; and Erickson and others, *Experiments in Head Start and Early Education.*

17. Victor Cicarelli and others, "The Impact of Head Start: An Evaluation of the Effects of Head Start in Children's Cognitive and Affective Development" (Westinghouse Learning Corp.–Ohio University, June 12, 1969; processed).

Bureau of the Budget and the Office of Economic Opportunity invited Head Start officials to give their views on implementing the recommendations of the report. One of the Westinghouse recommendations was accepted and implemented almost immediately: summer programs were converted to full-year programs, wherever possible, reducing the total number of children served by about half without changing the total budget. Head Start staff objected, however, to OEO's idea stemming from a second Westinghouse recommendation of converting all curricula to a few academically oriented models, considered to be documented successes, on the ground that there was insufficient evidence that a change should be made from the general child development model.

The Westinghouse report also called for Head Start to be more experimental. The Bureau of the Budget demanded that increased investments in experimental studies be accomplished within existing levels of expenditure. Head Start responded with a proposal for an experimental program to begin immediately with $2.5 million of existing funds allocated to the last three months of fiscal 1969 and expand to no less than $25.0 million by fiscal 1971. More emphasis on experimentation had been planned many months before the Westinghouse report appeared, but after the report's release, both the Bureau of the Budget and OEO increased the pressure for HSPV to become operational as an experimental, evaluated program.

In short order, then, several existing activities were converted into a planned variation project and presented to the Budget Bureau and OEO as a significant part of Head Start's response to the need for experimental programs. HSPV, therefore, had to begin as an experimental study as quickly as possible, and on a broad scale, converting as many operating sites as possible to experimental programs in fiscal 1969, 1970, and 1971.[18]

18. Excerpts from the presidential budget trace the policy expectations and the evaluation of HSPV: "In 1969 a significant portion of the grants will be used to try differing models of preschool instruction, especially those strongly emphasizing formal instruction, motivational techniques, and parent involvement." (*The Budget of the United States Government—Appendix, Fiscal Year 1969*, p. 98.) "In 1970, greater emphasis will be placed on experimentation through an estimated $25 million program of planned variation in Head Start using the Follow Through evaluation approach." (*Budget—Appendix, 1970*, p. 92.) "This program is a major element of the administration's emphasis on child development during the first 5 years of life. In 1970, it is estimated that local Head Start sponsors will continue to reduce summer programs in order to enroll more children in full-year and full-day programs. This is consistent with program evaluations which indicate longer and more noticeable re-

The feasibility of conducting a national experiment was hurriedly examined in May 1969. The problems of quasi-experimental designs, of identifying appropriate measures for different sponsors' outcomes, and of beginning data collection in a national field test in September 1969 were energetically discussed. Given a mutual Budget Bureau and Head Start management interest in experimenting rather than planning in fiscal 1969 and 1970—and the optimism of outside experts regarding quasi-experimental designs and measurement—the decision was made in early June 1969 to live with the risks and to proceed with evaluation of the sites selected between January and May for the HSPV demonstration effort.

The decision to begin experimental operations with the already-chosen sites and sponsors immediately had lasting consequences. Among these were an inability to reduce biases by applying available experimental designs to site, class, and child selection; the large number of sponsors representing unknown variations and heterogeneous outcomes, many of them difficult to measure; and inadequate planning for logistics, measurement, and analysis.

It seems likely that the study will contribute much to assessment methodology, to an understanding of what important preschool curricula provide to children, to the field of program implementation, and to the methodology of data analysis and reporting for interactive studies. The individual case studies, the sponsors' own studies, the dissemination experiments, and the cost analyses may add substantively to knowledge of child development and to national evaluation methodology. Sponsors and consultants have profited from the large-scale tests of curricula. Communities, parents, and teachers usually have welcomed HSPV programs and urged their continued support.

The study may not, however, add much information useful in improving federal education programs to that already available in 1969 from the comparative curriculum studies. This will be true particularly if, in the final analysis, the three-year study shows few differences among sponsors. The design as implemented may have so much "noise" in confounding outcome-related site and child characteristics with curricula

---

sults for full-year programs. Funding for experimental programs will reach $15 million in 1971, permitting expansion of testing and evaluation of different program models and some locally developed experimentation." (*Budget—Appendix, 1971*, p. 98.) "Under Head Start, new methods of providing developmental services to 3- to 5-year-old children will be demonstrated." (*Budget, 1973*, p. 132.)

that it simply cannot detect differential effects; or it may be that there are, in fact, few differential effects.

Final judgment on this matter must await 1971–72 findings and a full assessment of the analytic techniques and of the relationship of these HSPV data to Follow Through findings and to the findings from smaller, but more tightly designed comparative curriculum studies.[19]

### Influences on the Design of HSPV

What specific design decisions predetermined these limitations to HSPV as a policy study?

*Selection of models and sponsors.* Head Start Planned Variation began with sixteen sites and eight models.[20] The eight sponsors were chosen because their approaches were reasonably well defined, and their Follow Through models were fairly well implemented. Moreover, the models had been developed initially for disadvantaged preschool children and later extended upward to Follow Through, which argued for easier adaptation to Head Start than models that had been developed for older children. Research issues were not primary considerations in selecting the eight models.

If three or four distinctive and well-defined approaches had been chosen, to be replicated in a fairly large number of sites, the experimental design would have been stronger. Such a strategy, however, would have been somewhat at odds with the concept of a wide-ranging, try-it-out demonstration; and it would have required Follow Through to install models in new sites, to compensate for its own asymmetric design. Even with the best available experimental design, however, the selection of appropriate sponsors would have been on a best-guess basis, since there were no firm data to indicate what were the best settings or outcomes in a planned variation experiment.

The four models added in 1970 to meet the Budget Bureau's mandate of an experimental investment of $15 million included two in which the Head Start staff were interested; they were Follow Through approaches

19. Richard J. Light and Paul V. Smith, in "Accumulating Evidence: Procedures for Resolving Contradictions among Different Research Studies," *Harvard Educational Review,* vol. 41 (November 1971), pp. 429–71, suggest how policy decisions can be based on analysis of several studies that vary in design and measurement.

20. See note 27, p. 10, above.

featuring individual programming in early childhood education. A third was a pioneer among enrichment programs for low-income children and a leading example of humanistic approaches.[21] The fourth was a "non-model," in which early childhood specialists acted as educational advisers; they helped parents and staff to articulate their desires for the children and to devise projects to satisfy these locally selected goals.[22]

*Number of sites per sponsor.* In 1969, sponsors were asked to implement their models in as many sites as possible and HSPV hoped that by 1971 each sponsor would have at least four sites in operation. This was impossible since the HSPV sponsors did not have that many sites operating in Follow Through; one sponsor had only one Follow Through site, while others had more than five. The resulting asymmetry of the forty sites that twelve sponsors had put into operation by 1971 presented difficult analytical problems. Sorting out sponsor, site, and temporal effects in the comparisons of models demanded more time and money than were available to do the job; but, most important, there was simply no entirely satisfactory statistical way to recover from the limitations of the site selection process.

*Lack of random assignment.* All of the sites selected for HSVP were asked whether they were willing to have the Follow Through sponsor that was already in the community conduct a Head Start program. They were not given a choice of sponsors. All of those that were invited to participate in the study elected to do so. Public schools and parents of school-aged children had, of course, volunteered in 1967 or 1968 to participate in Follow Through and at that time had chosen the model for their community.

Since all of the HSPV sites agreed to participate when approached and thus were "volunteers," the program offers no basis for identifying a model or set of models that would be superior for all communities. For identifying a group of satisfactory models that communities could choose among, Follow Through would serve reasonably well, but HSPV would not offer statistically firm ground for generalization. Because of the pressure of time and the limited available funds, the combined Head Start–Follow Through program could be offered only in communities where Follow Through already was established.

---

21. See note 28, p. 10, above.

22. The Enabler (described on p. 10, above) cost per child per program-year was about $45 over regular Head Start costs; other sponsors' costs per child per year were about $350 in addition to regular Head Start yearly expenses.

Had there been time to plan the study properly, it is likely that a true experimental design would have been recommended. A design based on matched pairs or blocks might have permitted random selection of treatment sites and of comparison Head Start sites from among those volunteering for a model; it would have offered greater certainty that sponsor and site characteristics would not be confounded. The state of the art in 1969 would have made such a design possible.

*Comparison group design.* Whether the goal of the HSPV experiment was seen as the replacement of regular Head Start programs by new models or the offering of options to communities, the effectiveness of the new curricula had to be judged by comparison with the old. To omit the comparison would have been contrary both to the intent of the Budget Bureau, which had urged experimental programs to improve Head Start, and to the interests of Head Start personnel.

In 1969, considerable data on Head Start were available in the national evaluations that had begun in 1966. By 1971 the Educational Testing Service's longitudinal study would provide pre-program, post-program, and after-school-entry data for a sample of about 1,500 children. The thirty-four communities in the 1967 and 1968 national evaluations and the four in the longitudinal study, however, did not seem to provide an adequate geographic match for the planned variation sites. Also, since the data to be collected and procedures to be used for HSPV were uncertain, and Head Start programs themselves seemed to be changing, these earlier studies were not counted on as sources of comparative data.

From the beginning the object of the study was choosing among Head Start programs rather than between Head Start and "no Head Start." On the other hand, without normative measures for assessing the absolute level of child development, and with the possibility that no differences would be apparent among models or between experimental and regular Head Start programs, findings independent of outside control data could be interpreted as indicating that Head Start had no immediate benefits.

Locating true control children for Head Start programs was difficult. While the program nationally served only about 12 percent of all eligible children, the other 88 percent were not readily available as controls. In many sites Head Start programs served all eligible children. In rural areas the nonparticipants repeatedly were found to come from higher income, ineligible families. In other areas, Head Start recruited the least advantaged families or relatively higher income groups. In cities and densely populated areas, children who did not attend Head Start often took part in other preschool programs.

Locating similar sites without any Head Start or preschool program was even more difficult. Sites without Head Start often did not have community action programs either, or were politically different from communities that had sought and obtained federal funds for social action projects. In addition, Head Start staff felt that random selection for research purposes—"experimenting with our children"—was contrary to the program's philosophy. Recipients and staff tended to regard Head Start as a means of meeting the right of low-income children to some of the pleasant experiences in life that middle-income parents often provide for their children. In addition, they recalled bitterly headlines proclaiming that evaluators and researchers found their children "genetically inferior" or their program "a failure." Under these circumstances, requiring Head Start sites throughout the country to recruit control groups would have been unrealistic.

In the first two years of Head Start Planned Variation, only on-site comparisons were used. In 1971, off-site control children were added. The control sites were chosen for their high concentrations of children not enrolled in Head Start and for ethnic and age mixes that matched those of HSPV experimental groups. None of the HSPV communities offered large enough populations of the right age and ethnic mix to form an on-site control group.

*Off-site and on-site comparison classes.* Comparisons of experimental classes with other classes at the same site have the advantage of offering two groups for whom all conditions are similar. But comparisons with classes at other sites mean that there will be less diffusion and contamination between experimental and comparison classes. In Head Start it was difficult to segregate children, parents, and teachers in Planned Variation classes from the rest of the program. The experimental classes were required to meet the standards for health delivery, nutrition, social services, parent involvement, and other components not included in the HSPV curricula. Specialists in a site served all classes; HSPV could not afford to set up separate Head Start programs for each curriculum treatment.

But on-site diffusion did take place. Anecdotal evidence indicates that some sponsors tried to serve all the children they could reach; comparison classes in one of the best HSPV sites, with many classes, geographically separated, were contaminated in this way. At some sites, teachers who did not like the Planned Variation model were reassigned to comparison classes. And at almost all sites, some teachers were transferred between experimental and comparison classes, both during the school year and between years. At sites where classes were held in the same building, teachers in the experimental and comparison classes talked with each other about the program. Both the initial decision to use on-site comparisons where possible and the later adoption of a mixed strategy thus reflected the state of the art of field experimentation rather than political necessity.

*Study duration.* When HSPV was planned, one year was set aside to allow sponsors time to deliver their programs to a number of sites, a second year to consolidate teacher training, and the third year to assess the effects of a stabilized program. In 1969, neither a definition nor a measure of implementation was available, and no one knew how long it would take to achieve program stability under field conditions.

Had the pressure to expand an experimental program not existed, it is likely that HSPV would have been a one-year or possibly two-year informal demonstration. Fitting HSPV within the framework of a larger Head Start experimental program made it possible to test the value of the curricula under presumably stabilized conditions. It also made possible subsidiary studies of implementation, such as methodological research on the definition and measurement of implementation, analyses of how much time is required to implement each model, and whether or not most teachers could eventually learn the different approaches.

These analyses of implementation may be among the most useful findings for educational policy. For example, a model that only a few teachers could learn in three years' time would be a less valuable alternative for Head Start nationally than an equally effective model that could be reasonably well implemented by most teachers in one or two years. Implementation can now be assessed reasonably well for some models. The difficulties that various sponsors and teachers have in implementing programs can now be compared. The Budget Bureau demand for large experimental programs and the belief that at least three years would be needed for a fair test of HSPV coincided. Each year was costly, however; perhaps HSPV could have been operated for less time with little loss of results.

Until better data are available, study length will probably continue to be a major and expensive subject of controversy in social policy studies.

**Summary and Discussion**

The analysis of influences on key decisions regarding initiation of the HSPV study and aspects of the design could be extended to program management (for example, the choice of contractors), measurement of processes and outcomes, analytic approaches and reporting, and to utilization of research findings for Head Start policy, subsequent designs of experiments, and state and federal policies relating to early child development. Until such analyses are undertaken, conclusions regarding the influences on the HSPV design should not be generalized to these other areas.

With regard to the origins and design of HSPV, the pivotal decision was to transform a demonstration of how Follow Through and Head Start could work together into a national experiment on the effectiveness of different preschoool curricula. Expanding a demonstration program into an "experiment" and doing so in a very short time led to decisions regarding the choice of sites and sponsors from which there was no return.

If there were a statistical method that could cope with greater certainty with the confounding of sponsor and site characteristics, and if more were known about the basic dimensions of importance to preschool outcomes and how curricula differed on these dimensions, HSPV might have resulted in the strong inferences that are expected from a national experiment. Had the enthusiasm for getting the study operational in the fall of 1969 not so rapidly caused HSPV to turn into a new experimental program, good methodological solutions to design problems (some of which were within the state of the art in 1969) might have been utilized. One of the chief products of the HSPV analyses may be a more precise sense of what is and what is not negotiable in the design of a planned variation study.

The methodological and managerial circumstances under which the planned variation design may be most and least effective are only now becoming apparent. Those most favorable or least applicable for planned variation can guide future experiments.

*Methodological circumstances favoring the use of planned variation:* Each sponsor's objectives, and the procedures for reaching these objectives, are stated clearly and in detail. Some objectives, to be reached by different approaches, are common to all sponsors and can be measured with existing instruments. Procedures for field implementation are known to be effective, and techniques are available for assessing the extent of implementation. Variations among models in costs, or effectiveness (and probably in fundamental approach) are expected to be fairly large. Substantial differences in outcomes may be expected within three to five years. The time required before the program can be implemented under field conditions is known.

*Methodological circumstances unfavorable to the use of planned variation:* Various sponsors have substantially different goals and objectives, and few shared objectives. Instruments for measuring many major goals are unavailable, and the instruments that are available reflect goals unevenly. Sponsors' models are still in the development stage, so treatments keep changing. Variations in cost-effectiveness are probably trivial for decision making. Long-term implementation or long-term participation by individuals is required before substantial effects can be expected. The intervention has not been tried out in the field or on subjects to whom findings are to be generalized, and the time needed before the program can be implemented under field conditions is unknown.

*Managerial circumstances favoring the use of planned variation:* It is possible to lay down an adequate design for site selection, and all decision makers within a particular agency agree that a true experiment is the correct basis for policy decisions. Time is available to plan the study design, to develop and field test measures, and to prepare logistical support for data collection, and at least as much time, and resources, can be allocated to data analysis. Research personnel have a high degree of autonomy and relatively few higher levels of authority to go to for approval once the decision has been made to undertake the study. It is clear to all involved that the purpose of the study is research and experimentation, not service or program development.

*Managerial circumstances unfavorable to the use of planned variation:* Various policymaking and administrative levels have conflicting objectives. Design requirements must be sacrificed for lack of time or because of demands that conflict with experimentation. There is no systematic plan at the beginning of the project for using research findings in making policy decisions or modifying programs. Many layers of decision makers must concur prior to action being taken on designs, measures, analyses, and research management. Time and resources available for data analysis are inadequate. Uncertainty in the state of the art of intervention, design, measures, or analysis seems too high for the study to yield firm conclusions about the central policy question.

Through study of the Head Start and Follow Through experience, and analyses of similar social experiments, the requirements of the planned variation technique should be increasingly well defined. The requirements may well be more stringent than they were believed to be in 1969. Social researchers may have a surer sense of when they are justified in asserting that findings from imperfect designs and measures are better than no findings at all, and when they are on firm methodological grounds in advising that the full power of social experimentation techniques be applied to the policy questions on which the welfare of many people depends.

MARSHALL S. SMITH

# Evaluation Findings
# in Head Start
# Planned Variation

During the early months of 1969 the Office of Child
Development in the U.S. Department of Health, Education, and Welfare
planned a longitudinal study designed to assess the relative impact of a
variety of preschool curricula. The Head Start Planned Variation
(HSPV) study was to include three successive cohorts or "waves" of
children systematically assigned to specified preschool curricula, each
of which would be installed at two or more sites throughout the country.
The sites chosen were to meet three criteria:

• Sites were to be chosen from among those with on-going Head
Start programs and no funds were allocated for serving children other
than those already eligible to be served by Head Start.

• Each site was to draw participants from a preschool population
living largely within the attendance area of a school or schools where
older children attended a Follow Through program.

• Each site selected for HSPV had to agree to adopt the curriculum
model being used in the Follow Through schools in its area. Aid in implementing the models was provided by consultants responsible to the
original architects of the models. Since many of the Follow Through
curricula were adapted from programs originally designed for preschools,
the use of them at the preschool level was appropriate.

The design of the study called for children in all three waves to be
tested at the beginning and end of their Head Start experience. Following Head Start Planned Variation, a child would enter the Follow
Through program in his community and be evaluated at the beginning
and throughout his Follow Through experience. Records of the HSPV

101

and Follow Through evaluation could then be linked. The linkage would provide data for a longitudinal assessment of the combined preschool and early elementary experiences of the HSPV children. Testing was also arranged for other Head Start children in many planned variation sites. These children would attend regular Head Start classes, which did not have one of the designated curricula, and would serve as a local comparison group for the HSPV study (and eventually in the Follow Through evaluation). There were no non-Head Start controls.

In 1970–71, the second year of the Head Start Planned Variation experiment, thirty-seven Head Start sites used Planned Variation models. Eleven of the twelve models represented were preschool versions of models already installed in Follow Through.[1] Their sponsors' approaches spanned the range of educational theories from the behaviorist through the developmental. The twelfth model, the Enabler, was not descended from Follow Through but was a collection of community-oriented programs developed locally with HSPV assistance.[2] For most models there were comparison classes (usually more than one), some within the larger Head Start program, others outside it.

Nine of the twelve models had at least two sites with adequate comparison groups, and five had three sites, from which reasonable inferences can be drawn about model effects. The sites were not limited to one region of the country, though there was some regional concentration in some of the models (for example, the Florida Parent Education Model sites were all in the South); but most models were tried at a variety of locations.

### Measures Used in the Evaluation

Three distinct levels of testing were used in HSPV (see Table 1). Usually, about four classes at a site were selected for testing. Level I, which involved eight of the thirty-seven Planned Variation sites, was the most primitive, and no comparison groups were included in the testing. Information on children was gathered from their teachers, information about themselves from teachers and teacher aides, and ratings on the level of model implementation in the classrooms from sponsors and Head Start directors.

1. See notes 27 and 28, p. 10, above.
2. See p. 10, above.

**Table 1. Instruments Used in Head Start Planned Variation Evaluation, 1970–71**

| Level of evaluation and instrument | Data collection period | | |
|---|---|---|---|
|  | Fall | Mid-year | Spring |
| Level I |  |  |  |
| Child demographic information forms for each classroom, completed by teacher | x | ... | x |
| California Preschool Social Competency Scale for each child, completed by teacher | x | ... | x |
| Rating of level of implementation for each classroom, by sponsor | x | x | x |
| Rating of level of implementation for each site, by Head Start director | x | x | x |
| Self-survey of backgrounds and attitudes, by teacher and teacher aide | ... | ... | x |
| Level II (includes all activities in Level I) |  |  |  |
| Classroom observation, by trained evaluators | x | ... | x |
| Basic Child Test Battery[a] | x | ... | x |
| Ethnic Heritage Test, completed by child | x | ... | x |
| Level III (includes all activities in Levels I and II) |  |  |  |
| Stanford-Binet test for one-half of children, selected at random, in each classroom | x | ... | x |
| 8-Block Sort Task for other random half of children in each classroom | ... | ... | x |
| Parent interviews for parents of children taking 8-Block Sort Task | ... | ... | x |
| Intensive case studies, by University of Maryland | ... | ... | x |

Source: Deborah Walker, Mary Jo Bane, and Anthony Bryk, *The Quality of the Head Start Planned Variation Data* (Cambridge, Mass.: Huron Institute, 1973).
a. Pre-school Inventory; NYU Book 3D (pre-math, pre-science, and linguistic achievement); NYU Book 4A (letters, numerals, and prepositions); and Motor Inhibition Test.
... = Not applicable.

At Level II, comparison groups were also tested. Classroom observations by outside evaluators and tests of children's preschool skills and ethnic identification were added to the tests given at Level I. Eleven Planned Variation sites were in this group.

Four tests were added to the Level I and II tests at the eighteen Level III sites. One-half of the children chosen at random in each classroom were given an IQ test; the other half of the class were given a test of mother-child interaction, and a parent or guardian of each child completed a questionnaire on Head Start, the child, and the planned variation model.

Many of the large number of measures used to assess the cognitive characteristics of preschool youngsters appeared to be well constructed

and reliable.[3] By and large, however, the long-term predictive validity
of the measures is uncertain, for data are limited to correlations between
the results of tests given at preschool time and similar tests given in the
early elementary years. These correlations are generally moderate, falling
at most in the 0.40–0.50 range. One exception is the Stanford-Binet IQ
scores, which show a fair degree of internal stability from the preschool
years to late adolescence—the correlation of scores at age five and adult-
hood being in the range of 0.50–0.60.[4] Moreover, the Stanford-Binet
scores seem to be fairly strongly related to eventual years of schooling
completed. The correlation between IQ at age five and eventual years of
schooling is about 0.40.[5] For HSPV these data have an important draw-
back; the relationships were measured in the absence of effects of
preschools.

Whatever their limitations, the cognitive measures are far more reliable instruments than the noncognitive, which should be uniformly classified as experimental. Little is known about the reliability or validity of
noncognitive tests. Moreover, they have no clear relation to theory and
they raise severe administrative problems. In every instance the noncognitive measures used in HSPV seem inappropriate instruments for evaluating
the effects of a variety of models, a particular misfortune since the goals
of the sponsors in HSPV are so diverse.

By and large, no comprehensive norms or assessments of the psychometric characteristics of either cognitive or noncognitive measures exist
for the population of children served by Head Start.

### Analytical Strategy for HSPV

The analysis of HSPV focused principally on cognitive growth.
Though such analysis fails to capture much of the richness of a preschool
experience or the largest part of the differences among preschools, any
other analytical strategy would have seriously overplayed the value of
the data.

The shortcomings of the analysis are due in large part to the failure
to assign models randomly. Planned Variation sites were selected on

3. Deborah Walker, Mary Jo Bane, and Anthony Bryk, *The Quality of the Head
Start Planned Variation Data* (Cambridge, Mass.: Huron Institute, 1973). They
conducted the analyses for all three cohorts of HSPV.

4. Christopher Jencks and others, *Inequality: A Reassessment of the Effect of
Family and Schooling in America* (Basic Books, 1972), pp. 59 and 111.

5. Derived from ibid., pp. 111 and 337.

the basis of two criteria unrelated to the requirements for an adequate experimental design—that is, the presence of Head Start and of Follow Through. Not only was the local community given the opportunity to accept or reject the assigned curriculum, but it could choose the classes within a site that would use the Planned Variation curriculum. Comparison classes were chosen after the Planned Variation classes were selected, so that they can no more be described as random samples than the treatment classes. At two critical points—the assignment of curricula and the selection of treatment and comparisons—a fundamental rule of experimental design was violated.

If curricula had been randomly assigned to sites, then a comparison of treatments would yield unbiased estimates. If classes had been randomly distributed between Planned Variation and other groups within sites, then a comparison of the two would yield unbiased estimates. Or, if random samples of children from the same population—one group in a Head Start program, one not—had been taken, estimates of the general effects of a Head Start experience would be unbiased. Because none of the assignments were random, the estimates are biased in some unknown fashion. Estimating the effects thus becomes an art instead of a science.

Many statistical techniques—matching, covariance, blocking, crossed designs, standardization—can help reduce bias. Each may be helpful, but there is no way of determining which may be of greatest help. Consequently, it seemed judicious in the analysis of HSPV to use several of "the allowed principles of witchcraft."[6]

Not all the principles of methodological witchcraft were used in the HSPV evaluation, but several were. The data must be interpreted cautiously, for most of the effects are small and somewhat sensitive to the analytical strategy used.[7] Presumably, those large effects that turn out

6. John W. Tukey, "Discussion on temporal changes in treatment-effect correlation," in Gene V. Glass, *Proceedings of the 1970 Invitational Conference on Testing Problems* (Princeton, N.J.: Educational Testing Service, 1971).

7. The analysis concentrated on the classroom unit, but data on individuals, sites, and models were examined to determine whether aggregation to different levels influenced the size of the estimated effects. To reduce bias in the analysis, cross-tabulation, covariance adjustment, and matching were used to estimate the adjustments on dependent variables needed to compensate for initial differences among treatment and comparison groups. Models were compared both directly and indirectly, the latter being comparisons of the differences between various models at the site level and their control groups at the same site. A mixture of these techniques was used in hopes of creating a variety of corroborative analyses. Marshall S. Smith, *Some Short Term Effects of Project Head Start: A Report on the Second Year of Planned Variation—1970–71* (Cambridge, Mass.: Huron Institute, 1973), chap. 5.

to be insensitive to variation in method of analysis should inspire confidence.

## Summary of Findings in Main Effects Study

Three main questions were addressed in the Head Start Planned Variation study:

• What are the overall short-term effects on children of a Head Start experience?

• Are there discernible differences between the effects on children of a Head Start Planned Variation experience and a conventional Head Start experience?

• Do Planned Variation models differ, one from the other, in their effects on Head Start children?

### Short-term Effects of the Head Start Experience

The Head Start experience substantially increased children's test scores on all five outcome measures. On four of the five, children's scores doubled or tripled the natural rate of growth over the seven or eight months of the Head Start program (see Table 2). On the fifth measure, the Stanford-Binet, the scores of children in the sample would have naturally fallen by about 0.30 standard deviation;[8] the Head Start experience not only arrested this expected decrease but raised the participants' Stanford-Binet scores by roughly 0.35 standard deviation.

Those children with prior preschool experience gained less overall than did children for whom Head Start was the first year of preschool; but the Head Start effects for the two groups were about equal.[9] Thus the expected natural growth is less for children with prior preschool experience than for those without. Children who entered first grade directly from Head Start tended to gain more on the four cognitive tests than children who entered kindergarten directly from Head Start.[10] There

8. That is, their observed IQ on this standardized test would have declined by about 5 points.

9. See Smith, *Some Short Term Effects,* chap. 4.

10. A number of sites (particularly in the Southeast) do not have kindergartens. In these sites Head Start children generally go directly from Head Start into first grade.

**Table 2. Effects of Head Start as Measured by Cognitive Tests, 1970–71**

| | Gain in test scores[a] | | |
|---|---|---|---|
| Test | Total | Attributed to maturation | Attributed to Head Start |
| Basic Child Test Battery | | | |
| Preschool Inventory | 0.942 | 0.496 | 0.446 |
| Book 3D | 0.727 | 0.363 | 0.364 |
| Book 4A | 1.151 | 0.333 | 0.818 |
| Motor Inhibition | 0.36 | 0.10 | 0.26 |
| Stanford-Binet | 0.348 | −0.296 | 0.644 |

Source: Marshall S. Smith, *Some Short Term Effects of Project Head Start: A Report on the Second Year of Planned Variation—1970–71* (Huron Institute, 1973).

a. To determine the gains attributable to Head Start, the children were divided into twelve groups by ethnic background, preschool experience, and entering grade. Their scores on all five cognitive tests were dependent variables in a series of sixty regression equations run on the twelve groups. The independent variables were age, sex, family income, household size, mother's education, and a set of dummy variables to control for data that were missing. One product of these equations was a set of prediction coefficients for each of the independent variables. If the main difference between the scores of children entering the program at forty-eight months of age and fifty-six months of age is reflected in the coefficient for age for the particular age groups, then a child's expected score due to maturation can be estimated from the coefficient. The difference between the estimated score and the child's actual score at the end of the program can be attributed to Head Start. Scores in this table are group means derived from the estimated scores and actual scores. Gains may be slightly unrealistic because the child's experience in taking the test before the program may affect his score at the end and because the coefficients for age may be biased. The gains are expressed in the metric of the standard deviation of pre-tests.

seem to be no consistent differences among Mexican-American, black, and white children in their Head Start gains on the five outcomes.

### Differences in Effects between Planned Variation and Conventional Head Start Programs

The question whether there are overall differences in effects between Planned Variation and conventional Head Start programs seems, on reflection, to be of little importance. Differences might be expected among Planned Variation programs but there is little reason to expect systematic differences between the overall Planned Variation and conventional programs. This question, like many questions about the impact of the whole program, completely obscures systematic differences among treatments.

The only reason for questioning the difference is to determine whether the extra funds allocated to HSPV programs (approximately $350 per child) had a consistent effect on the measured outcomes. This study, like a large number of recent research efforts, failed to detect any systematic relationship of gross expenditures to outcomes. There seem to be no differences in effects between the Planned Variation program as a whole and the comparison Head Start groups on any of the five outcome measures.

### Differential Effects of the Various Planned Variation Models

As was expected, there were few strong differences among the Planned Variation models in effectiveness (see Table 3). On each of the outcome measures, the majority of the models are average in effectiveness. Moreover, none stand out as more or less effective than the others on more than two of the five outcome measures. There are, to put it bluntly, no overall winners or losers. The more tentative expectation that models that emphasized academic drill, combined with systematic reinforcement, would be more effective than others was realized for only one of the four cognitive measures, the Book 4A measure which assesses knowledge of letters, numerals, and shape names. The Behavior Analysis Approach is clearly superior to all the other models and to the comparison classes in its effectiveness in raising Book 4A test scores. The Englemann-Becker Model and the Individualized Early Learning Program instruction emphasize academic drill and both appear to be above average in their impact on the basis of this test. On the other cognitive tests, however, there is no strong indication that these three models are especially effective.

Other researchers in the preschool area[11] have found that structured academic emphasis and drill on cognitive tests may have a generally positive effect. The data on Head Start Planned Variation, however, indicate that the effect is specific rather than general—that this approach may be more effective for imparting information that is easily taught through systematic drill than in other cognitive areas.

One model clearly stands out as more effective than the others in raising Stanford-Binet test scores. The High/Scope Model appears to increase individual Stanford-Binet scores by an estimated twelve to fifteen points, or 0.90 standard deviation. In other Planned Variation models and comparison classes, Stanford-Binet scores increased three to four points, or roughly 0.20 standard deviation. The estimates of the

11. Joan S. Bissell, "The Cognitive Effects of Pre-school Programs for Disadvantaged Children" (doctoral dissertation, Harvard University, 1970); Sheldon H. White and others, *Federal Programs for Young Children: Review and Recommendations,* 4 vols. (U.S. Government Printing Office, 1973).

**Table 3. Summary of Head Start Planned Variation Model
Effectiveness on Outcome Measures, 1970–71**

|  | Basic Child Test Battery | | | | |
|---|---|---|---|---|---|
| Model[a] | Book 3D | Book 4A | Preschool Inventory | Motor Inhibition | Stanford-Binet |
| Responsive Educational Program | 0 | 0 | 0 | 0 | 0 |
| Tucson Early Education Model | 0 | 0 | 0 | 0 | 0 |
| Bank Street College of Education Approach | 0 | 0 | 0 | + | − |
| Englemann-Becker Model | 0 | + | 0 | 0 | 0 |
| Behavior Analysis Approach | 0 | ++ | 0 | 0 | 0 |
| High/Scope Model | + | 0 | 0 | 0 | ++ |
| Florida Parent Education Model | − | 0 | 0 | 0 | 0 |
| EDC Open Education Program | 0 | 0 | 0 | 0 | 0 |
| Individualized Early Learning Program | 0 | + | 0 | − | + |
| Responsive Environments Corp. Early Childhood Model | − | − | 0 | 0 | + |
| Enabler Model | 0 | − | 0 | + | b |

Source: Smith, *Some Short Term Effects.*
a. No results are reported for the Independent Learning Model because its only site received no Level II or Level III testing.
b. Test not administered.
0 = average effectiveness.
− = below average effectiveness.
+ = above average effectiveness.
++ = highly effective.

High/Scope effects not only reflect findings at two very different sites but findings observed in an earlier cohort.[12] The gains apparently apply over the entire range of Stanford-Binet items.[13]

Two of the eleven models (Individualized Early Learning Program and Responsive Environments Corporation Early Childhood Model) were responsible for 40 percent of the instances where effectiveness on an outcome measure was other than average. The significance of these outcomes is questionable, for both are one-site tests. Even in test-by-test

12. Helen Featherstone, *Cognitive Effects of Pre-school Programs on Different Types of Children* (Huron Institute, 1973).
13. See John Butler, "Item Component of Preschool IQ Gain" (Harvard Graduate School of Education, 1973; processed). There is some indication that the High/Scope Model may also be of above average effectiveness on Book 3D, but no firm conclusion can be reached from the data.

analysis, important differences in model effectiveness may be concealed. All models, for example, show average effectiveness on the Preschool Inventory Test, an unexpected result since this test is probably the most reliable of the measures used. The lack of clear differences, however, probably reflects the nature of the test itself, which was developed to assess the overall impact of preschool training on children. It attempts to measure a wide range of skills and is thus relatively insensitive to particular differences among curricula.

### Interactions with Child Characteristics

To determine whether models might affect different children in different and important ways, the clear main effects of each model were carefully examined. Though the models that showed substantial effects were not equally successful for all types of children, there were no major disordinal interactions between model and child—that is, no model that was effective on the average for a certain test was particularly effective for one type of child and particularly ineffective for another.

In another exploration of the interaction of child and model characteristics, both 1969–70 and 1970–71 data on the Preschool Inventory and the Stanford-Binet tests were examined.[14] Many interactions were observed, but with one exception there was no stability over the two years. Most of the patterns of interaction reflected in the outcome measures were different in the two years. The single significant and repeated interaction, where the characteristics of children had clear impact on their performance on given curricula, showed up on a behavioral scoring system applied to the Stanford-Binet results.[15] Children were categorized before the test according to their "passivity" and "competence." Passivity was indicated by a child's remaining silent and passive if he did not know the answer to an item, competence by his attempting to answer items he was unfamiliar with and elaborating on correct answers. Children were classified as high or low on these two measures. In both years two general tendencies were discovered: "more competent" and "less passive" children were more successful in the "less directive" models, and "less compe-

14. Featherstone, *Cognitive Effects of Pre-school Programs.*

15. Developed by Margaret E. Hertzig and others, "Class and Ethnic Differences in the Responsiveness of Preschool Children to Cognitive Demands," Monograph 33 (1) (Society for Research in Child Development, 1968).

tent" and "more passive" children were more successful in the "more directive" models.[16]

## Conclusions

Numerous studies have shown that Head Start has a clear and strong short-term effect on cognitive outcomes.[17] And many more studies of school effects indicate that it is unlikely that any one curriculum will show a clear advantage over others in producing cognitive growth.[18] However, the effects of some HSPV models do persist. There seems to be a clear relation between the goals and child outcomes of the academically oriented curricula on the test of letters and numbers, of the High/Scope Model on the Stanford-Binet test, and of the "directive models" with younger, "more passive," and generally less ready children.

These findings indicate that evaluations of preschool (and school) curricula should attend more to the goals of the curricula than to the psychometric characteristics of the measures. This, of course, is not an easy task when noncognitive measures are at issue. Until tests have been devised that can truly assess and compare progress toward well-understood goals, at least a diversity of cognitively oriented measures should be used in making program assessments.

16. Using the second-year data, and grouping the models by broad similarities to add power to the analysis, it is possible to make some additional provocative hypotheses. Two "more directive" or "adult controlled" models—the Englemann-Becker Model and the Behavior Analysis Approach—tended to favor children without preschool experience, children who initially score on the low end of the distribution in the Preschool Inventory Test, boys with preschool experience in contrast to girls with preschool experience, and younger children. Three "less directed" and "student initiated" models—the EDC Open Education Program, the Bank Street College of Education Approach, and the Responsive Educational Program—favored children with preschool experience (on the Preschool Inventory Test only) and initially high-scoring children. These findings apply only to the second year, but they appear to be consistent both internally and with the two-year findings on passivity.

17. Lois-ellin Datta, "A Report on Evaluation Studies of Project Head Start" (paper presented at the 1969 American Psychological Association convention, September 1969; processed); and Marian S. Stearns, *Report on Preschool Programs: The Effects of Preschool Programs on Disadvantaged Children and Their Families* (U.S. Department of Health, Education, and Welfare, Office of Child Development, 1971).

18. Jencks and others, *Inequality: A Reassessment.*

CAROL VANDEUSEN LUKAS

# Problems in Implementing Head Start Planned Variation Models

Head Start Planned Variation (HSPV) was designed to investigate "the impact of various well-defined educational environments and learning situations on the Head Start child."[1] It is not surprising, therefore, that most analyses of the program have been devoted to testing child outcomes on a variety of measures. One additional issue in testing effectiveness, however, is deciding whether the models are actually being used in the classrooms. The question of model implementation is important to the interpretation of the results of the experiment.[2] Ideally, a test of treatment effectiveness is unambiguous: the treatment being tested is clearly defined and is the cause of the results that are found. Furthermore, the findings can be generalized to other situations.[3] Attaining this ideal requires fully implemented treatments, with full implementation defined as exact replication—every experimental situation is an identical example of the treatment. This definition implies not only that treatments should be fully present, but that they should be carefully specified. To look only at treatment outcomes, then, implies that implementation is assumed not to be a problem—that all models are fully, or at least equally, implemented.

1. U.S. Department of Health, Education, and Welfare, Office of Child Development, *Head Start Planned Variation Study* (1970), p. 1.
2. This discussion is based on Carol VanDeusen Lukas and Cynthia Wohlleb, "Implementation of Head Start Planned Variation: 1970–71" (Cambridge, Mass.: Huron Institute, 1973).
3. These issues are usually implemented under what Campbell and Stanley call internal and external validity. Donald T. Campbell and Julian C. Stanley, *Experimental and Quasi-Experimental Designs for Research* (Rand McNally, 1963), p. 5.

While this assumption might be justified in a laboratory study where the treatment can be expected to be in place because the researcher has extensive control over the experimental situation, it cannot be made in a social experiment like HSPV. In this study, sponsors installed their programs, not in nearby laboratory schools, but in distant Head Start sites, where they could offer only intermittent training and supervision. A large number of people were involved in implementing the models, and the process was therefore often beyond the researcher's control.

It would be unwise, then, to act on the assumption that treatments have been implemented without checking on it—unless the treatment effects are robust. If the treatments show strong effects, it might be argued that deviations from the ideally implemented treatment do not create serious problems because the interpretation is still clear. Finding that treatment effects exist in spite of treatment ambiguity and variation in implementation is in fact desirable for administrators who want to disseminate the programs. Robust treatments suggest that the effects will exist regardless of the conditions under which the programs are instituted.

In most cases, however, treatment effects are not strong, but weak and variable. Interpretation is then complicated if the treatment has been only partially implemented. When it is not clear what form of a treatment is actually being tested, it is difficult to know whether weak effects result from poor theory or from the fact that the treatment was never actually tried. Similarly, when the requirements for the ideal situation are not met, it is difficult in the face of variable effects to determine whether a treatment would be successful in a particular new site. In general, then, it is important to know whether treatments are being used successfully.

In planning Head Start Planned Variation it was recognized that the full implementation of treatments was important and that it could not be taken for granted. It was realized that the sponsors would need time to get their programs going, and that some sponsors might take longer than others to transfer their models to particular sites. It was assumed, however, that all models would be fully implemented by the third year of the study.[4] The study of implementation was conceived primarily as a check

4. An Office of Child Development publication states, "We are not looking forward to completion of the Planned Variation study with full implementation in 1971–72." *Head Start Planned Variation Study*, p. 3.

on this assumption, not as a major component of HSPV. A portion of that study—the data from its second year, 1970–71—is the focus of this paper.

## To What Extent Are the Treatments Implemented?

The primary measure of the extent of implementation in the second year of Head Start Planned Variation was ratings of teacher performance by the model sponsors. Each sponsor was asked to rate the performance of every head teacher in his model on a scale running from not acceptable (0), to barely acceptable (1, 2, 3), to average (4, 5, 6), to outstanding (7, 8, 9). Sponsors' judgments were based on their personal conception of their programs rather than on shared standards of implementation. Since it cannot be assumed that all sponsors used the instrument in the same way, comparisons across models are unwarranted; the measure cannot be used to show that one model was implemented to a greater extent than another. More important, the lack of shared standards means that the criteria for the sponsors' judgments are unknown. The rating scale is not anchored by an explicit definition of what constitutes "outstanding" implementation. The meaning of "average" is unclear, and there is no indication of how large or how important the intervals of the scale are in relation to full implementation. One result of these shortcomings is that the sponsors' ratings are difficult to interpret. More generally, since the sponsor ratings are essentially the only direct measure of implementation for the second year, they indicate that the study was conducted without an agreed upon standard of what constitutes full implementation. Thus comparisons of the extent of implementation can only be relative: one teacher may be rated more highly than another, but how their classes compare to the ideal of full implementation cannot be determined. It is impossible to judge whether the level of implementation is high enough for a class to be considered a valid test of a model.

The sponsor ratings, despite their shortcomings, reveal that all models were considered by their sponsors to be moderately well implemented in the winter of the second year of the study: the mean ratings for each model ranged from 4.8 to 7.0 (see Table 1). More important, though, is the fact that the level of implementation varied substantially among sites implementing the same model (as shown by the large site standard deviations). Analysis of this variation (see Table 2) shows that the differences among models are not significant but that the differences among sites

**Table 1.  Sponsor Ratings of Implementation of Head Start Planned
Variation Models, by Classrooms at Each Site**

| Model and site | Mean rating | Standard deviation | Number of classrooms |
|---|---|---|---|
| Responsive Educational Program | 5.0 | 2.30 | 27 |
| Buffalo | 4.2 | 2.99 | 6 |
| Duluth | 4.4 | 2.45 | 8 |
| Fresno | 4.0 | 1.41 | 4 |
| Salt Lake | 6.2 | 1.50 | 4 |
| Tacoma | 6.8 | 1.10 | 5 |
| Tucson Early Education Model | a | a | a |
| Bank Street College of Education Approach | 4.8 | 1.81 | 32 |
| Boulder | 4.5 | 2.08 | 4 |
| Tuskegee | 4.0 | 1.96 | 13 |
| Wilmington | 5.5 | 0.93 | 8 |
| Elmira | 5.4 | 1.90 | 7 |
| Englemann-Becker Model | 5.6 | 1.50 | 16 |
| East St. Louis | 6.0 | 1.63 | 7 |
| Tupelo | 6.3 | 1.53 | 3 |
| East Las Vegas | 4.8 | 1.17 | 6 |
| Behavior Analysis Approach | a | a | a |
| High/Scope Model | 4.9 | 1.39 | 31 |
| Fort Walton Beach | 5.0 | 1.58 | 5 |
| Central Oz | 5.0 | 1.41 | 16 |
| Greeley | 5.2 | 0.96 | 4 |
| Seattle | 4.5 | 1.64 | 6 |
| Florida Parent Education Model | 5.2 | 2.13 | 18 |
| Jacksonville | 4.0 | 0.00 | 1 |
| Jonesboro | 5.0 | 0.00 | 3 |
| Chattanooga | 6.4 | 0.53 | 9 |
| Houston | 2.8 | 3.20 | 5 |
| EDC Open Education Program | a | a | a |
| Individualized Early Learning Program: Lock Haven | 5.0 | 0.58 | 7 |
| Responsive Environments Corp. Early Childhood Model: Kansas City | 7.0 | 0.76 | 8 |
| Interdependent Learning Model: Virgin Islands | a | a | a |
| Enabler Model | 5.2 | 1.53 | 28 |
| Billings | 4.6 | 1.34 | 5 |
| Colorado Springs | 5.8 | 2.14 | 6 |
| Bellows Falls | 6.2 | 1.17 | 6 |
| Newburgh | 4.8 | 1.39 | 8 |
| Puerto Rico | 4.6 | 0.58 | 3 |

Source: Carol VanDeusen Lukas and Cynthia Wohlleb, "Implementation of Head Start Planned Variation: 1970-71," pt. 1 (Cambridge, Mass.: Huron Institute, 1973), p. 40. The mean ratings and standard
deviations are based on all available data.
   a. No data available.

**Table 2. Analysis of Variance on Sponsor Ratings of Teachers in Head Start Planned Variation Models**[a]

| Source of variance | df | Mean square | F-test | Significance | Percent of total sum of squares |
|---|---|---|---|---|---|
| Model | 5 | 2.144 | 0.339 | 0.500 | 3.13 |
| Site within model | 12 | 6.321 | 2.076 | 0.028 | 22.15 |
| Class within site[b] | 84 | 3.045 | ... | | 74.72 |
| Total | 99 | 3.390 | | | 100.00 |

a. The analysis is based on a balanced design with six models and eighteen sites. An unweighted means analysis of variance is used to approximate the solution with an unequal number of classes within the sites; since sites are nested within models, the effects of a site cannot be separated from the effects of the site in interaction with the model.

b. Indicates the effect used in testing the preceding effect; because sites are considered as fixed factors, class within site is used to test both sites and models.

within the same model are. This suggests that although one sponsor's ratings are not consistently higher than another's, the sponsors do distinguish among sites within their models as to how well their model is being implemented.

Approximately 74 percent of the variance in ratings lies within sites. This means that most of the differences in levels of implementation are among teachers within sites; in general, in all sites some teachers are better than others in performing the model. That variation exists within models, both among and within sites, then, indicates that the experimental treatments vary across classrooms representing each model, at least according to their sponsors.

While the sponsors' impressions cannot be objectively verified, they are partially corroborated by data collected with the Classroom Observation Instrument (COI), a standardized instrument designed by the Stanford Research Institute to record child and adult behavior and interactions in HSPV and Follow Through.[5] The COI records the frequency of such vari-

5. The Classroom Observation Instrument was not used as a primary measure of implementation because it was used in only a subsample of HSPV classes and the variables available for analysis failed to tap the important dimensions of all models. The variables are based on observations that record overt behavior and require rapid coding. They include factors such as the frequency of academic activity, of children asking questions, of independent play, or of working in small groups. There are no variables that reflect the context or purpose of behavior, such as whether a teacher is responsive to the children's needs, whether a child is alert and interested in the classroom activity, or whether a child makes discoveries on his own. Thus a model that specifies particular types of activities and interactions can be studied more adequately with this measure than one that emphasizes the purpose and context of behavior.

ables as overall academic activity, independent child activity, and teacher and aide participation in various activities. Analysis of the frequency patterns of such activities[6] indicates that some models can be distinguished on a few important dimensions. The Englemann-Becker Model and the Behavior Analysis Approach, in keeping with their theories, have high frequencies on academic activity. Also, as would be expected, the Bank Street College of Education Approach and the Individualized Early Learning Program show much independent child activity, and while the former is low on adult acknowledgment, praise, and feedback, the latter is high on adult acknowledgment and adult asking thought questions. Only these four models can easily be distinguished. While the other models may in fact be similar in practice, it is also possible that there are differences among them that are not picked up with this instrument.

The COI analyses also reveal a great deal of variation within the models among classrooms. This variation indicates that the treatments really are not uniform, confirming the variation found in the sponsor ratings of level of implementation.

It appears, then, that some teachers are implementing the treatments better than others and that classes under the same treatment label have differing experiences. Although some models can be distinguished from the others on important dimensions, it seems clear that the ideal of identically replicated treatments has not been met. Moreover, since there is no clear standard of implementation, there is no way of determining how far the variations are from being acceptable examples of the treatments under examination.

## Why Is There Variation in Implementation?

It is important to understand the determinants of variation in implementation in order to take them into account in planning future studies. One possibility is that the variation merely reflects differences in the length of time teachers have worked with a model: the longer a teacher works with a model, the higher the level of implementation should be. Although 1970–71 was the second year of the experiment, some sites were

6. See Lukas and Wohlleb, "Implementation of Head Start Planned Variation," and Marian S. Stearns, Kathryn A. Preecs, and Gerald T. Steinmetz, "Classroom Observation Study of Implementation in Head Start Planned Variation, 1970–1971" (Menlo Park, Calif.: Stanford Research Institute, 1973).

participating for the first time, and even in second-year sites there were new teachers in the program. But comparisons of first- and second-year sites and teachers through analyses of variance reveal no effects of length of participation. The ratings for second-year sites and teachers are not significantly higher than those for first-year, nor are ratings in May significantly higher than ratings in February.[7] Not only does this finding indicate that length of participation does not explain the variation in level of implementation, but it calls into question the commonly accepted assumption that time and exposure to a curriculum will ultimately result in full implementation.

A competing view of the causes of variation in implementation holds that the variation stems from the nature of the treatments and the nature of the implementation process. Treatments may fail to be replicated because they are not specified in behavioral terms.[8] If a model is to be replicated, the activity that should go on in that program must be made explicit and described in detail. Otherwise, the teacher does not have enough information to make her classroom exactly like another's on the relevant dimensions.

The HSPV models were not fully specified because most of them were not adequately developed when the study began and some were not complete when it ended. Moreover, all of the models changed during the course of the experiment. While the changes may have been educationally desirable, they may have led to differences in implementation both because treatments that are constantly changing are hard to define and because models may evolve in different ways at different sites.[9]

The lack of behavioral specifications for the treatments also results from the nature of some models. Even if all models were complete in the sense of being firmly based on clear and integrated theories of how to teach children, some of the sponsors still would not be able to provide detailed operational descriptions of day-to-day classroom activity because their philosophy runs counter to close prescription. Instead they set out

7. See Lukas and Wohlleb, "Implementation of Head Start Planned Variation," tables 4, 6, and C-1.

8. See Anne Monaghan, "An Exploratory Study of the Match Between Classroom Practice and Educational Theory: Models in Head Start Planned Variation" (Cambridge, Mass.: Huron Institute, 1973), for a description of her attempts to specify the models during the final year of HSPV.

9. Failure to have well-defined models in HSPV is a result of the state of the art of educational theory and not the result of sponsors' failure to take the experiment seriously. The models included in the study were reportedly the best available approaches to early childhood education when the study began.

general principles and encourage teachers to carry them out in the manner that best fits their style and the needs of their students.

The absence of behavioral specifications for models, then, may be a cause of variation in implementation, especially for models that are incomplete or that encourage local adaptation. Although this explanation seems reasonable, it could not be tested empirically in HSPV because the implementation measures were model-specific. In making their ratings, the sponsors may have taken the model ambiguities into account so that the scale intervals have no consistent meaning from model to model.

Assuming that the relationships described here are correct, however, two predictions can be made about the occurrence of variation in implementation. In programs where the lack of specification results from the incompleteness of the program, variation ought to be reduced as theory advances and the program is refined. But where the lack of specification is inherent in the nature of the model, variation in implementation will continue to occur. For these models, replication is an inappropriate standard.

Implementation varies also because, quite simply, it depends on a large number of people. Treatment replication would require that all teaching staffs, after receiving training in a model, be equally able and motivated to implement the treatment. But that requirement is not realistic in a program like HSPV. A conception of the implementation process must acknowledge differing levels of skills, histories, values, and competing interests and priorities—not only of individuals but of the organizations in which they work.

This is not to say that the sponsor's contribution at a site is not an important factor in the implementation process. The sponsor's staff is the primary source of information about the model and the quality and extent of their training, together with such personal factors as their commitment to the site, will affect implementation. But the local staff and the site organization also may influence implementation. The assignment of teachers to a new curriculum will not automatically result in full implementation, even if the model is complete and the training is good. Their implementation of a program depends on a complex set of factors, such as their opinion of the model, their previous methods of instruction, how long they have been teaching, and the level of their teaching skills. The organization in which the teachers work is also influential. If they must worry about funding problems or conflicts with the staff, for example, they may not be able to devote their full energies to implementing a new educational program; or if the director makes demands on the staff that interfere with the model's requirements, implementation may suffer. Moreover, since the HSPV sites are Head Start sites that existed before the study, implementation may also be influenced by the sites' established norms and operating procedures. The staffs may or may not be receptive to new ideas; they may have goals and interests that take precedence over model implementation. Thus, the variety of factors that influence implementation may explain differences in implementation.

This interactive view of the implementation process is supported by reports of early childhood experts who monitored the implementation of HSPV treatments for the Office of Child Development, and by other studies of innovations and discussions of organizational and decision-making theory.[10]

To test hypotheses about factors affecting implementation, sponsors' ratings of their models' implementation at the site and classroom levels (there was no appreciable variation in implementation between models) were used as the dependent measure in a series of regression analyses. Although the analyses were based on data collected for other purposes and did not include many potentially important variables, the resulting equations are informative. At the site level, an equation using sponsors' assessments of the level of intrastaff friction, of the rapport between the staff and the administration, and of the adequacy of the physical plant resulted in a multiple $R^2$ of 0.977. In other words, these characteristics explain more than 97 percent of the site-to-site variation in implementation as estimated by sponsors. The inescapable conclusion is that at the site level, sponsors are equating the pleasantness of a site with the level of implementation there.

Extensive analyses at the classroom level, controlling for the three atmosphere variables, suggest that such factors as teacher characteristics and training, while having some influence on implementation, explain only

10. See, for example, Neal C. Gross, Joseph B. Giacquinta, and Marilyn Bernstein, *Implementing Organizational Innovations: A Sociological Analysis of Planned Educational Change* (Basic Books, 1971); Louis M. Smith and Patricia M. Keith, *Anatomy of Educational Innovation: An Organizational Analysis of an Elementary School* (Wiley, 1971); W. W. Charters, Jr., and others, *The Process of Planned Change in the School's Instructional Organization* (University of Oregon, Center for the Advanced Study of Educational Administration, 1973); Graham T. Allison, *Essence of Decision: Explaining the Cuban Missile Crisis* (Little, Brown, 1971); Walter Williams, *Social Policy Research and Analysis: The Experience in the Federal Social Agencies* (American Elsevier, 1971).

about 10 percent of the variation within sites.[11] The regression analyses, then, though they do not account for all the variation, support the idea that both staff and site factors influence implementation.

Thus, it appears that the degree of model implementation is determined not simply by length of exposure to a model but by a variety of processes and treatment factors. Variation results because some treatments have not been completely developed and some by their nature encourage variation. Variation also occurs because the people putting the curriculum into action differ in their skills and in their feelings about the model, as determined both by their own backgrounds and by the norms and priorities of their organizations. Given this view that implementation varies according to the nature of the situation, the standard of identical replication of sponsors' models may be unrealistic. In any study involving complex treatments and depending on local people for implementation, some individuals will undoubtedly implement the treatment better than others. Also, where local adaptation of sponsors' principles is encouraged, it seems inappropriate that "full implementation" should call for experimental classes that look exactly like the model.

### Conclusions

Program implementation data from the second year of HSPV reveal: (1) The treatments, as they are implemented in the classrooms, are not identical replications of a well-specified model. As a result, the interpretation of treatment effects will not be as "clean" as it ideally ought to be. (2) The study was conducted without an agreed upon definition of implementation. Since the extent of implementation varies, this is a serious flaw. Without the definition as a criterion, the adequacy of implementation in a particular class cannot be evaluated. (3) The nature of some models indicates that it is inappropriate to define implementation in terms of identical replication. (4) Variation in implementation is a function of the nature of the implementation process. The lack of relationship between time and implementation together with the interactive view of the process suggests that variation in implementation is inevitable and that the expectation that all treatments will eventually reach full implementation is unrealistic.

11. Lukas and Wohlleb, "Implementation of Head Start Planned Variation," pt. 1, table 32, p. 192.

These findings do not mean that social experiments are not worthwhile. They do suggest, however, while variation within treatments ought to be minimized, some variation is inevitable. Two conclusions follow:

*Alternative standards for a valid experiment must be developed.* Since exact replication appears to be an inappropriate standard for judging the adequacy of implementation, alternative standards must be developed if useful conclusions are to be drawn about the effectiveness of treatments. Full implementation must be realistically defined and differences in implementation must be taken into account in analyzing treatment effectiveness. A redefinition of full implementation must admit some variation among classes, for the sponsor and the teaching staff may adapt a model to the unique situation in a site, or even a class within a site, and to changes in a situation over time. Even in those models that do not emphasize adaptation, exact replication should not be expected. And yet, there must be limits to the variation. There must be some gauge of the amount of variation that can exist in a fully implemented example of a model, as well as a point at which the variation is so great that the implementation becomes partial and another point at which implementation is so minimal that there is no evidence of the model. Until limits of variation for all models are defined—and in some models this may be impossible—there can be no operational definition of full implementation.

It is also important that differences in implementation be included in the outcome analyses because some classes undoubtedly will be less than fully implemented even if implementation is redefined. A teacher, for example, may use only portions of a model or use the model only part of the time. Such differences can be taken into account by setting a criterion level —the level of implementation regarded as acceptable for the treatment— and analyzing effects only in classes that exceed that level. Essentially the distinction would be between treatment and no treatment. The critical issue in making this simple distinction would be deciding where the cut-off point should be. Again, it is not clear how to go about this or whether it is possible for all models.

This approach, however, potentially sacrifices a great deal of data. Another approach—using implementation as a covariate or as an independent variable in a regression equation to control for the variation in effects that result from differences in implementation—would make use of all available data. But it is important that the scales used to measure the extent of implementation be anchored so that standards for judgments, particularly the criteria for full implementation, are made explicit. The problem of comparing partial implementation must also be resolved. Within a single model, a class in which the treatment is, say, 60 percent implemented may not look like another in which the treatment is 60 percent implemented because different parts of the model may be present in each. Criteria must be established to determine when these classes can be considered to be acceptable replications of a single treatment. Such criteria depend on a good definition of implementation; without that definition it is impossible to include level of implementation as a covariate in the analysis of experimental outcomes.

All these standards must be set in order to provide a basis for determining whether a treatment as implemented is an acceptable example of the treatment to be tested. If standards cannot be established—for example, if limits cannot be set on variation, at least to the extent of differentiating model classes from nonmodel classes and specifying what the model classes have in common—then there is no basis for determining whether treatments are valid.

*The process of implementation is, in itself, an important topic for study.* In a traditional experimental framework, research focuses on the effect of treatments, and the study of implementation serves primarily as a simple check on the presence of the treatments. When it cannot be assumed that all classes will reach full implementation, it is equally important to find out whether particular treatments can be implemented, and in what form, and to identify the factors that determine the process.

This paper has presented analyses, using data originally collected for other purposes, of individual factors that might affect implementation. What is needed now is a study of the implementation process: a study designed to ask what effects sponsors' involvement, training efforts, and staff organization had; to ask what characteristics of the local staff, of the Head Start organization, and of the community in which the center is located affect implementation; and to develop a theory of how these factors are interrelated—that is, to develop a theory of process rather than of individual factors. Either studies of natural variation in delivery systems or experiments with specified strategies may be useful. This type of study goes beyond the issue of experimental validity to an investigation of conceptions of planned change. Literature on innovations, intervention theory, organizations, and decision making will be useful in further probing these issues.

Among the persistent problems in a study of innovation is the ambiguous and changing nature of the innovation itself. Description is difficult because the process is elusive: participants, not surprisingly, tend to be unclear about what they are to do or why they are to do it. Also, no two situations are alike. If the innovation process is in fact the result of a complex interaction, those factors that determine implementation under one set of cirmucstances may be somewhat, or entirely, different from those under another set. Consequently, attempts to specify universal determinants of implementation should be viewed with caution.

MARSHALL S. SMITH

# Design Strategies
# for Experimental Studies

In designing a strategy to improve the effectiveness of schools, educational treatments should be identified that are consistently associated with desired changes in student outcomes—curricula or teaching methods or modes of school organization that produce higher student test scores or satisfaction or other measures of success. To accomplish this goal requires thinking through at least three sets of problems. The first problem is that of defining educational treatments: what level of complexity of treatment is appropriate to an analysis designed to yield useful results on the effectiveness of schooling? The second problem is that of validity: what steps should be taken to insure that educational treatments shown to be effective can be implemented elsewhere? A third set of problems involves measurement: what instruments should be used to measure both school outcomes and school influences?

## Defining Educational Treatments

Clearly the education system is extraordinarily complex. Teachers, principals, curricula, materials, attitudes, and other factors influence student outcomes, interacting among themselves and with other complicated systems—home, community, labor market. To identify ways of improving the effectiveness of schools, the characteristics of the education system that are related to student outcomes and the kinds of changes in them that might improve outcomes must be isolated.

It is impossible to estimate the impact of the whole education system on children, for there is no available comparison group of children who do not go to school, nor does there exist a way to create such a group. Even if a random sample of children were excluded from schools for purposes of observing their intellectual skills and behavior, each member would still be living in a community in which going to school was a normal thing to do. The question is moot anyway, because no one seriously advocates a policy of abolishing schools.

Even analyzing major subsystems of education (kindergarten, high school) seems unlikely to yield fruitful knowledge of the impact of education on students. There are not likely to be similar students outside the subsystem, and those within are bound to encounter tremendous diversity in teaching method, curriculum, teacher qualification and attitude, and so on. Since the question is one of how to improve the effectiveness of education, finding out the average impact of those subsystems, even if this were possible, would not be nearly as useful as discovering the relationship between particular efforts and outcomes.

At the other extreme are the easily measurable elements[1] of the education system—for example, characteristics of teaching behavior, such as frequency of positive reinforcement, or of classrooms and schools, such as pupil-teacher ratio. A great many studies focused on such elements have failed to find strong or stable relationships between them and child outcomes. Pupil-teacher ratios, for example, are not by themselves good predictors of student outcomes; but it does not seem reasonable to expect their effects to be independent of the educational environment in which they are imbedded. The effect of class size is bound to depend on the teacher's approach, the curriculum, the teaching materials, the school's organization, and so forth.

But if "everything affects everything else," then every aspect of environment, including local politics and the weather, would have to be controlled in a fruitful research endeavor. Some intermediate level of treatments—*programs* that are configurations of elements thought to be significant—may, however, have identifiable effects on outcomes inde-

---

1. A crude hierarchy of terms is used here to distinguish among different levels of educational interventions. *Elements* refer to identifiable characteristics such as classroom size or teacher attributes—characteristics that by and of themselves bear little direct or obvious relation to student outcomes. *Programs* are configurations of elements that have some theoretical coherence and that taken as a whole have an arguable relation to outcomes. *Systems* and *subsystems* are haphazard sets of programs. The principal interest here is on detecting and explaining effects of programs. Both the term *intervention* and the term *treatment* are used to refer to any of the three levels.

pendent of the larger context in which they are carried out, and would thus be expected to have a particular effect on student outcomes under a variety of conditions in different parts of the country.

Rather than assessing the impact of whole *systems* or the effect of particular elements, research should be aimed at identifying or developing manageable educational programs and investigating their relationship to child outcomes under varying conditions. Since it is not feasible to field test large numbers of programs, a strategy for gathering useful information about the effectiveness of schools should concentrate further on programs that have a reasonable theoretical base and are composed of elements that affect children directly.

Research on particular elements of education has been conducted in a vacuum where neither the kind of outcome nor the impact of change has been predictable. Research on programs should offer a rationale for why a particular set of elements should combine to produce a particular set of outcomes for the students. Moreover, before any large-scale field testing is done, the levels that the outcomes of a successful program should reach and the time necessary to reach them should be specified.

The programs chosen for attention should be configurations of elements that directly affect student outcomes. For example, the relationships of teachers in the teachers' room or the power of parents or school board members in decision making are not elements that affect students directly. These elements may indeed be important, but it can be presumed that they affect child outcomes through their effect on more immediate elements such as a choice of curriculum or teachers' behavior *in* the classroom.

## Three Types of Validity

As important as the choice of a program aimed at improving the effectiveness of schools is the establishment of procedures for estimating its effects. The estimates of the effects of programs on child outcomes should be valid both in terms of the experiment and beyond the experiment.

If the results of an educational program are to be attributed to the treatment specified, they must clearly not have arisen from something other than the treatment. The internal validity of the experiment depends on evidence that the treatment was responsible for the effect. Thus a true experiment must involve not only the group that receives the treatment, but another similar one that does not. Then the uncontrolled elements in the experiment—other school influences, influences in the home, biological maturation—are presumed to be common to both groups.

*Internal validity* rests on the degree of assurance with which it can be said that the treatment group differs from the control group only in having been exposed to the treatment. Systematic initial differences between the groups other than exposure to the treatment represent rival explanations for differences in outcome.

Estimates of the effects of a treatment can be termed unbiased to the extent that the effects of such confounding influences are eliminated. It is possible to physically control for those outside influences either by limiting the types of subjects in the samples or by distributing such influences equally between the two groups. For example, in estimating the effect of a particular Follow Through model in which sex, social class, or attendance at out-of-school tutoring programs were possible confounding influences, the treatment and control samples might be restricted to middle-class males who do not attend after-school tutoring sessions. Or the two samples might be composed of similar proportions of males, subjects in the middle class, and subjects who attend after-school tutoring sessions.

Needless to say, the very large number of plausible confounding influences limits the usefulness of physical control and makes statistical control attractive. The confounding influences that are apparent can be measured and their relation to the outcome estimated; the estimated effect of the treatment can then be adjusted to reflect the differences in these factors between the experimental and control groups. Again, however, all of the plausible rival influences may not be accounted for.

That problem can be skirted by assigning subjects randomly to experimental and control groups prior to the onset of the experiment. Thus the expected difference among the groups is zero on every influence but the treatment. There will, of course, always be differences among groups on potentially important rival characteristics, but if the assignment process is truly random and the samples are large, the differences probably will be relatively unimportant.

The use of probability statistics for estimating the statistical significance of effects of an experiment rests in part on the assumption that confounding influences have been successfully controlled. Studies in which subjects are randomly assigned to experimental and control groups as a means of controlling for confounding influences are known as *true experiments,* while those that employ the less reliable means of control are known as *quasi-experiments.*

The *external validity* of an experiment depends on whether the statistical inferences made from samples can be accepted as extending to a larger population. To estimate arithmetic achievement levels among eighteen-year-olds in the United States, for example, would depend on testing a representative sample of eighteen-year-olds. Confidence about the similarity between the sample distribution and the actual population distribution would increase as the size of the sample increased. A sample survey of this sort can also provide general descriptions of changes within the population, but no direct information about what caused the changes.

The distribution of the effects of educational influences, say, of a particular Head Start program on children, could be estimated in a similar way. After the population of Head Start centers in the country had been defined, a probability sample could be drawn. Children at the centers would be randomly assigned to treatment (the particular program) and control groups. At the end of the Head Start year their outcomes on particular items would be measured. The general effect of the program on children would be the result of the pooled results of the various centers. The random assignment of children makes each center experiment internally valid, and the probability sample of centers assures the external validity of the experiment aimed at determining the overall average effect of a program. But this example of an externally valid experiment does not respond to the question of why the outcomes of a program will vary from one location to another. In order to explain this variation and to make inferences about the probable effects of the program in new settings, it is necessary to understand the program itself.

The third factor that governs the validity of inferences about a program's results is therefore its implementation.[2] Only prior and complete specification of the "important" elements and interactions among elements in a program will make possible the measurement of its implementation. Variations in outcomes of the programs in different locations can result from weaknesses in the specifications or theory underlying a

2. For more extended discussion of the implementation problem, see Carol Van-Deusen Lukas, "Problems in Implementing Head Start Planned Variation Models," pp. 113–25, above.

program, from the context in which the program is employed, or from the lack of integrity in the program's implementation. Reliable predictions of the possibilities of duplicating the effects of a program depend as much on knowledge of these factors as on the internal and external validity of the experiment.

## Two Kinds of Measurement Problems

Any experimental program has not only intended effects, whose desired outcomes should be carefully specified, but unintended consequences. And often an experiment includes a variety of program designs that are intended to produce somewhat different outcomes. It seems reasonable then to assess each program with its own appropriate measure as well as measures generally appropriate to the variety of programs. It might eventually be possible to construct profiles of the impacts of the various programs and contrast them. Most educational programs, however, have no clearly specified criteria for evaluation, and only the most straightforward cognitive outcomes can be measured with any assurance of accuracy.

Most research on the effects of schools has relied on norm-referenced standardized tests of achievement to measure outcomes. These tests of cognitive skills are intended to be appropriate across a wide variety of curriculum approaches—tests of very early reading achievement, for example, commonly contain a smattering of items intended to assess word-attack skills (phonics and structural analysis), reading knowledge of very commonly used words both separately and in short sentences (sight reading), and general language orientation (picture vocabulary). The items in the test are also selected to insure that the tests do not discriminate against certain kinds of children.

In order to encompass most of the major curriculum strategies the tests must be designed so that overall scores will not differ for different curricular approaches. The need to be appropriate to many programs may force the tests to be inappropriate for distinguishing among particular programs. Yet the tests must demonstrate acceptable levels of reliability and predictive validity in order to sell. They do this by measuring children's competence in particular areas, perhaps those that curriculum developers do not expect children to master. This may explain why the results of most research on the effects of schools suggest that differences among schools are not very important while differences among experiences outside of school are. Reliable tests that are insensitive to differences among programs must be sensitive to differences among children that are either innate or the result of extracurricular experience.

To be sure, standardized tests of achievement are not always insensitive to differences among curricula. Large and powerful differences among clear-cut approaches to education cause significant and important differences in standardized test scores, at least in the short run.[3] But if the differences among curricula are in areas largely ignored by the tests, they will not be reflected in the scores.

A rigorously designed educational program and a discriminating measurement instrument are two of the necessary characteristics of a useful study. A third requirement is an appropriate strategy for gathering information. Actually putting a program into operation is by far the most useful strategy, for it insures that all the influences in the educational setting will be known. An ideal experiment would provide for establishing a program and then observing it in operation. But observing programs that are already in operation also permits examination of the educational environment. Both strategies require a carefully designed inquiry into the operating characteristics of a program and a search for potentially important confounding educational influences. In most research on schools, such probes are impossible. Direct observational methods will have to be employed in research if the effects of educational programs are ever to be understood.

The most widely used and by far the weakest method of measuring the extent of different educational influences is the questionnaire, which attempts to assess both the existence and degree of implementation of a program and the existence and quality of other potential influences. Typically, such data on school influences are gathered from teachers and principals. The questions must be aimed at specific observable elements in the school setting, and from them the analyst must piece together configurations representing particular programs. The task is extremely difficult and ordinarily deteriorates into an analysis of elements as though they were programs.

The elements, of course, may not have been accurately measured, and schools consequently cannot be reliably designated as representing

3. See pp. 110–11, above, and Marvin G. Cline and others, *Education as Experimentation: Evaluation of the Follow Through Planned Variation Model: Early Effects of Follow Through* (Cambridge, Mass.: Abt Associates, Inc., 1974).

different program treatments. If a substantial amount of misallocation occurs, differences among schools on the outcome measures will be unreliable.

Any study that relies on answers to a questionnaire as a means of defining treatments should include some measure of the questionnaire's reliability. At least for a small sample of respondents, data should be gathered twice and compared. Also, each element of the treatment might be measured in a number of ways.

The study will be fundamentally in error if treatments are not validly specified. In Coleman's survey of equality of educational opportunity,[4] for example, it is impossible to associate particular students with particular teachers or, in general, with other internal characteristics of the school. In analyses of the data, students are all assumed to be receiving homogeneous treatments within their schools—the school, in effect, is a program rather than a system. Yet, different children in the same school clearly do not have equal access to the resources, and they are treated in different ways. Defining a school as a program reduces the fidelity of the treatment definition and leads to a misclassification of programs and thus a shrinking of the differences among treatments.

Equally distorting in the comparison of programs is systematic bias in the responses to questionnaire items. Teachers and principals may be motivated to assess their own or their schools' characteristics in a more positive light than they should. Teachers, for example, may overestimate the time they spend with students, and principals may overestimate the quality of the science labs. A general overestimation or underestimation will lead to misidentification of programs and consequently to the attenuation of effect estimates.

Survey questionnaires for assessing the effects of the educational environment are not only weak but potentially misleading. They exaggerate all the questions of validity—does the program exist, to what degree has it been implemented, can its effects be applied generally, what outside influences skew its results? Direct observation is a far more reliable way of assessing the desired effects of programs as well as the impact of other elements in their environment. And direct observation of a program that has been carefully designed to test specific educational treatments is most likely to yield useful results.

4. James S. Coleman and others, *Equality of Educational Opportunity*, U.S. Department of Health, Education, and Welfare, Office of Education (1966).

## Recent Large-Scale Field Studies

In recent years a substantial number of large-scale educational studies has been undertaken and considerable effort has gone into using the data produced to make inferences about the effectiveness of schools. Unfortunately, many of the studies have failed to accord with so many of the demands of a valid social experiment that their usefulness as a basis for improving school effectiveness is extremely limited. *Systems assessments* which examine a cross-section of the student population principally yield descriptive information. *Longitudinal assessments* are little better for making judgments about the effectiveness of education programs. *Systems impact studies* have produced more useful information, for control groups have sometimes been included in these evaluations. *Exploratory evaluations of programs* that seem to fit the experimental requirements have also been useful because they include control groups. Potentially the most productive studies are *developmental program evaluations,* which assign a variety of treatments that can be tested. As the design and evaluation problems in these most sophisticated studies are reduced, the ability to prescribe effective educational action will grow.

### System Assessment Studies

The purpose of a system assessment is to describe and provide accounting information about the natural status of an entire education system—for example, the entire public elementary education system in the United States. By definition, every unit eligible for assessment is included in the system; thus, true control groups are not possible. Similarly, by definition neither the system nor any of its parts is manipulated for the purpose of the study; no attempt is made to assign different programs to units of the system.

The lack of control groups forecloses the possibility of separating the effects of the system from the effects of outside influences. The lack of control over programs means that programs must be identified while they are occurring, and they will often be inaccurately identified. It means also that the measured effects of the different programs are confounded by other educational influences and the characteristics of the students.

Because of these weaknesses, little significance can be attached to inferences about school effects from such a major assessment as the Coleman report.[5] The principal conclusion of that national survey was that, with the exception of the social class composition of the student body, variations in educational inputs bore little relation to variations in outcomes once the effect of family and background influences had been removed. Subsequent analyses suggested that even when those effects were not removed, there was little relation between variations in input and variations in effect.

Public reaction to this conclusion ranged from complete skepticism to complete acceptance. Some interpreters went so far as to state that the study showed that "schools don't make a difference" and used the data to argue that schooling was not important to the teaching of educational skills.

This interpretation should be ruled out altogether. The lack of control groups (out-of-school children) in the survey made it impossible to assess the effect of schools on children. Only differences among the effects of various treatments could be contrasted. But differing treatments were not assigned, implemented, or systematically sampled, and the least reliable measuring instrument—teacher, principal, and superintendent questionnaires—was used to define treatments. Moreover, the study did little to prevent biases in the estimates of treatment effects from outside influences and student characteristics.

Taking a number of measures over a period of time (as the Plowden and Project Talent studies did) does not appear to increase the ability to determine treatment effects.[6] A measure taken before the study begins only provides another control for individual differences and in the absence of good knowledge about the nature of the treatments may falsely inspire confidence in inherently bad data. Moreover, a variety of individual measures that can be assessed simultaneously can fill the same role, especially in studies where treatments are measured at an

5. Ibid.

6. This may seem a radical statement, and it should certainly be tested. Analyses of data gathered before and after the programs could be compared to analyses of data on the same subjects gathered only at the end. If there turned out to be no difference in the estimated effects of the treatments, future study designers might save themselves some money and time. For data on the programs see Gilbert F. Peaker, *The Plowden Children Four Years Later* (Slough, England: National Foundation for Educational Research, 1971); John C. Flanagan and William W. Cooley, *Project Talent: One-Year Follow-up Studies* (University of Pittsburgh, Project Talent, 1966); Cline and others, *Education as Experimentation;* and p. 104, above.

aggregate level. The variation in aggregated outcome achievement scores is often as much explained by social class aggregated over all students in a school, for example, as it is explained by aggregated achievement scores on tests taken before the treatment began.

In theory no variable that might make a significant contribution to explaining the effect of a model should be eliminated. Yet for most system assessment studies, measures taken before the studies begin may simply be a waste of time and energy.

The problems of identifying programs from questionnaires or even from general observational techniques cancel much of the usefulness of assessments for detecting program effects. When combined with the problems of uncontrolled differences among subjects and other interacting influences, they seem insurmountable.

Assessment studies should only be used to describe the general relation of a system to some external norm or criterion. In the National Assessment of Educational Progress, for example, no attention is paid to any effects of educational experiences on the subjects other than the length of schooling. As the tests are repeated, they will provide some general descriptive information about changes in the level of competence in the society, which in turn might be generally traced to overall national policy.

Other important information might also come from longitudinal assessment studies. Sophisticated models like those of Duncan and Jencks relating gross characteristics of children's background, character, and education to later outcomes depend on a great deal of data about patterns of mental growth, determinants of career choices, and so forth. Such data are derived primarily from assessments of the impact of systems on individuals.[7]

### System Evaluation Studies

System evaluation studies seek to measure the impact of a governmental intervention, such as Head Start or Title I of the Elementary and Secondary Education Act, on the children served—to judge the quality of the intervention as a whole. They share many of the design defi-

---

7. See Otis Dudley Duncan, David L. Featherman, and Beverly Duncan, *Socioeconomic Background and Occupational Achievement: Extensions of a Basic Model,* U.S. Office of Education, Final Report, Project 5-0074 (EO-191), Contract OE-5-85-072 (1968); and Christopher S. Jencks and others, *Inequality: A Reassessment of the Effect of Family and Schooling in America* (Basic Books, 1972).

ciencies of system assessment studies: neither attempts to implement particular treatments or to assign subjects to treatment and control groups. Impact evaluation studies of programs universally applied to the target population suffer from the same limitations as assessment studies. The lack of control groups precludes information about overall system effects, and the effects of individual treatments are confounded to an unknown extent by influences from other treatments and by their subjects' exposure to the treatments. They consequently yield only descriptive information and suggested points for further study.

Only when a general intervention is a scarce resource, not available to an entire target population, is there a possibility of having a control group of eligible students not participating in the system against which participants can be compared. In the Westinghouse-Ohio study of the impact of Head Start,[8] for example, it was possible to construct pseudo control groups and to attempt an assessment of the overall impact of the intervention on the children.

An evaluation of the saturated system, where a control group is theoretically impossible (though sometimes contrived), must rely on a specified criterion or a noncontemporary reference group that can serve as a proxy for a control group. If a criterion is adopted beforehand as the measurement device, a simple representative sample of system participants could be drawn and their participation in the system might be verified, but no tests of their initial levels of achievement would be necessary. When a criterion level is specified in advance of a study, some notion about what percentages of participants ought to reach or exceed that level would probably have been developed. A substantial deviation from that goal could constitute success or failure of the intervention.

The only serious difficulties in carrying out such a study lie in the planning stages. Some decisions would have to be made about the appropriate domains to test; for a system designed, say, to educate poor children, this might be a very difficult task. Guidelines would allow a great latitude of acceptable treatments, and it would be difficult to argue for consistent measures across the whole system. One way out of that quandary would be to select certain domains, such as reading or art, thought to be important and then to assess only those sites where the treatment was appropriate. This, however, would require carrying out

8. Victor Cicarelli and others, "The Impact of Head Start: An Evaluation of the Effects of Head Start on Children's Cognitive and Affective Development" (Westinghouse Learning Corp.–Ohio University, June 12, 1969; processed).

a census in order to determine which treatments were appropriate for inclusion in the study, a task that might prove unmanageable. It also suggests a contradiction, for the simple impact study would now involve the detection of appropriate treatments and, consequently, the selection of subsamples of the population and the matching of appropriate test domains to them. And even if those problems are set aside by testing all children on all parts, the task of attempting to define the criteria to determine success remains.

If a noncontemporary reference group were to be used for control, it would be necessary to find a way to gather the relevant information. One possibility is within a series of assessment studies. The outcomes for participants in the system being evaluated would be contrasted with outcomes for similar children who were assessed at the same ages before and after the intervention occurred.

Constructing a substitute for a control group in an intervention where not all eligibles are served also presents problems. In many locations the people eligible for the limited spaces include those who wanted to be and were selected and those who were *not* selected, some of whom wanted to be and some of whom did not want to be in the intervention.

Those who did not want to be in the intervention are clearly biased as candidates for a comparison group. If those who wanted to be included were excluded by lottery, they would be an appropriate control group. If, however, they were excluded on a "first come, first served" basis, or for some undefined reason, their appropriateness as controls would be open to question. And if they were excluded because they were clearly less needy of the intervention, they would be clearly inappropriate controls. If it were uncertain whether those who wanted to participate were appropriate as controls, it would probably be well to form a control group out of them along with a control group from those who did not want to participate. The two control groups, with some luck, might roughly isolate the effect of "wanting to participate in the system."

Often there is no alternative to forming a nonrandom control group. When this occurs, analysts often face the question of whether or not to use matching as a device to control confounding influences. Where there is no matching, a census or a random sample of the nonparticipating eligibles might be used as a control group. Should the two groups' characteristics as an aggregate not match, then statistical adjustments would have to be made in the analysis to obtain approximately unbiased treatment estimates. Matching requires selecting individuals for the control group whose characteristics are similar to those of the treatment group.

It is possible that estimated differences between matched groups will be inaccurate because of errors in matching. Only advances in theory can reduce the chances that inappropriate variables will be chosen to match groups from two different populations. But if the reliability of the match between treatment and control groups is in question, either a number of variables or a number of measurements of a single variable can be used to make the match. Once the appropriate steps have been taken to assure reliability, differences in covariables between the two populations can be estimated and the amount of bias due to the outside influences that are potentially most harmful can be isolated.[9] Constructing a control group through this rather complicated maneuver has substantial advantages over using a substitute for the control group. Careful matching should eliminate a great deal of bias in the estimation of effects, though it certainly cannot reduce all bias.[10]

Even at that, system impact studies certainly do not hold much promise of revealing anything about the effects of a treatment that is less general than an overall system.

### Exploratory Program Evaluations

The possibility of manipulating programs and assigning subjects is also missing in exploratory program evaluations. In these studies, how-

9. One of the key issues seen by critics of matching and of adjustment procedures like covariance is the selection of a proper measure of reliability. Donald T. Campbell and Albert Erlenbacher, in "How Regression Artifacts in Quasi-Experimental Evaluations Can Mistakenly Make Compensatory Education Look Harmful," in Jerome Hellmuth (ed.), *Compensatory Education: A National Debate*, vol. 3 of *Disadvantaged Child* (Brunner/Mazel, 1970), pp. 185–210, suggest that in covariance analysis a pretest covariate should be corrected until the within-groups regression coefficient is equal to one. (This is a slight oversimplification of their suggestion.) Their procedure results essentially in a gain-score analysis, like Lord's of the early sixties (see F. M. Lord, "A Paradox in the Interpretation of Group Comparisons," *Psychological Bulletin*, vol. 72 [1969], pp. 336–37). As in Lord's paradox, it is misspecification of the equation predicting the variation in the dependent variable rather than unreliability, at least as defined in any conventional manner, that causes the problems. A proper approach, therefore, would be to attempt to accurately specify the equation rather than to arbitrarily adjust the regression coefficient used in the covariance analysis.

10. See Donald Rubin, *Matching to Remove Bias in Observational Studies*, Technical Report 33 (Harvard University, Department of Statistics, 1970); and Marshall S. Smith, *Some Short Term Effects of Project Head Start: A Report on the Second Year of Planned Variation—1970–71* (Huron Institute, 1973).

ever, the focus is not on describing an entire system or on estimating its overall impact. Rather the purpose is to suggest what the impact of a system might be if certain exemplary programs were universally implemented. Thus, attention centers on distinguishing among naturally occurring programs.

These studies are aimed at finding exemplary treatments—on the positive, or negative, end of an output dimension. Because the assignment of treatments and subjects is not controlled, statistical techniques have to be used to overcome confounding influences. Nonetheless, the focus of the studies on identifying programs and the chances of utilizing control groups raise the possibility that some important indication of effective programs may be detected.

An easy way to survey the field for treatments that has shown positive effects is to rely on results reported in the popular and professional literature. The *AIR—It Works* evaluation of compensatory education programs ferreted out demonstration treatments in this way.[11] Observers were then dispatched to the treatment sites to gather information and report on their inner workings. The first set of descriptions of the treatments included about fifty termed "exemplary" on the basis of effects measured in what appeared to approximate internally valid studies.

No attempt is made in such evaluations to assess the external validity of a program, and the measured effects may be confined to one site. And the survey may, of course, overlook effective but ill-publicized programs.

In every distribution of treatment effects, some will appear to be particularly positive just by chance, and such effects ordinarily disappear in later assessments. This seems to be exactly what happened to roughly 75 percent of the treatments identified by AIR; the effects were greatly reduced when evaluations were carried out the following year.[12] Nonetheless, the study did point to some types of treatments that may prove in the long run to be systematically related to outcomes. In particular, one conclusion from several of the exemplary programs was that highly structured reading curricula with an emphasis on drill produce strong

11. See David G. Hawkridge, Albert B. Chalupsky, and A. Oscar H. Roberts, *A Study of Selected Exemplary Programs for the Education of Disadvantaged Children*, pts. 1 and 2 (Palo Alto, Calif.: American Institutes for Research in the Behavioral Sciences, 1968).

12. Other methodological problems stemming from inconsistencies in local evaluations or from the problems associated with program impact and assessment studies might have helped to create this drastic reduction.

effects on reading achievement. The Follow Through evaluation indicates that the conclusion may be valid.[13] A finding of this sort is an argument for further study, perhaps introducing into the search for exemplary programs some theoretical notions about the kinds of programs to look for and a uniform method for evaluating those discovered.

Exploratory evaluation studies may be very effective pre-experimental studies. They could turn up one or two particularly effective treatments that could be put quickly to a more rigorous experimental test, with several replications, for the same cost as a single test for many treatments. This may be a worthwhile tradeoff. Although a natural variations design is certainly not an appropriate test of external validity, it offers an operating milieu closer to reality than does planned variation. In Head Start Planned Variation, for example, extra money, help, and training were used in the implementation of treatments. Thus the results of HSPV can, in theory, only be generalized to new situations where the same support services exist.

### Developmental Program Evaluation

Developmental program evaluations call for treatments to be systematically assigned to location, and subjects to be systematically assigned to treatment or to control group status. Generally, in practice, neither the treatments nor the treatment and control groups are assigned randomly by community or by smaller units of analysis. The studies are thus quasi-experimental, lying somewhere between a true experiment and a natural experiment.

While such studies might yield information about the effectiveness of particular practices, they usually merely point to the kinds of practices that might be productive. Moreover, one of their important functions presumably is to provide information to improve the quality of the programs. Both Follow Through and Head Start Planned Variation, however, have offered more help in the development of programs than in the estimation of their effects.

Field experiments share the general methodological characteristics of developmental program evaluations; programs are implemented in assigned sites, and subjects within the sites can be systematically assigned to treatment and control status. Experience with these studies is not extensive as yet. Two recent experiments, however, that fit this category

13. See Cline and others, *Education as Experimentation.*

—each lasting only one year—are the Performance Contracting experiment and the Teacher Incentives experiment.[14]

The critical advantage of this kind of study over the assessment and evaluation studies is the opportunity it provides to assign treatments to locations and control the implementation of the treatments, and to assign subjects at the treatment sites to either treatment or control status. In theory, these studies avoid most of the methodological shortcomings of the other studies. In practice, however, they are not so efficient, for the problems of assigning, defining, and implementing treatments make their conclusions only suggestive evidence of treatment effects.

### Problems in the Definition and Implementation of Treatments

Lack of a clear theoretical understanding of the different treatments used in past studies has caused as many problems as has a faulty assignment process. Without a theory about the potential effect of the various treatments as a guide, both the form and the timing of the assessment of all treatments have followed a uniform schedule. Not only might such a schedule force premature estimates of potential effects, but it may also be damaging to a spirit of educational innovation.

Consider an open classroom curriculum like the EDC Open Education Program or the Bank Street College of Education Approach.[15] These approaches raise a variety of problems for the evaluators. One of their aims is to provide a child with a free and stimulating environment in the classroom so that he may develop the self-confidence and self-motivation to address himself to learning problems. To a large extent, the child is self-pacing; faced with a learning task, he exercises some control over the speed and approach he takes. There is strong theoretical support for the method, yet neither the theory nor the various adaptations explain when, on what measures, to what degree, and for how long effects should be detected. Should children initially be assessed on measures of self-confidence and motivation and not measured on their reading success? Should some of the supposed side benefits of the approaches, such as creativity, be assessed? Not only are appropriate

14. See U.S. Office of Economic Opportunity, Office of Planning, Research, and Evaluation, *An Experiment in Performance Contracting* (1972); and Planar Corp., *Incentives in Education Project, Impact Evaluation Report. Final Report* (Washington, D.C.: Planar Corp., 1972).

15. See descriptions of the programs on pp. 6–7, above.

instruments to tap these areas lacking, but again there is no guide to indicate when and how much of an effect should be expected.

The Englemann-Becker Model, on the other hand, is based on a theory—still primitive—that directly predicts effects of a large magnitude on standardized tests of achievement. Moreover, it predicts that the effects will occur a short time after the treatment is initiated and will be detectable long after the intervention has been completed, though the latter point is less precise than the former. With this information it is possible to make a careful and reasonably precise evaluation. But to contrast either of the other approaches to this one and thereby run the risk of rejecting one of the other strategies may be a grave error.

Most planned variation experiments also founder because of the general lack of knowledge about the process of implementation, and particularly about how to measure implementation. With no means of assuring that treatments are adhering to well-defined operating patterns, and limited confidence in the methods and timing of program measurements, there seems very little justification for an evaluation. No matter how careful the design, or how sophisticated the analysis, every conclusion will be questionable. On the one hand, there will be no assurance that the evaluation instruments are being used in a theoretically justifiable manner, and on the other, no barometer to indicate how lack of control over implementation may be influencing outcomes. By chance, one treatment might show one or more consistently strong and positive effects in an evaluation.

The problem of evaluation may be partially circumvented if more information can be gathered on two areas that compromise the studies. Implementation is unfortunately an unlikely candidate because it may only be studied in a continuing large-scale field experiment. The development of adequate theories and empirical data about the expected effects of proposed interventions, though an extremely difficult task, seems necessary. It involves a retreat to laboratory and small-scale field studies and finally a reexamination of the underlying assumptions of treatments.

The only HSPV and Follow Through models that have been developed along such lines are the Englemann-Becker, Individualized Early Learning, High/Scope, and Behavior Analysis approaches.[16] For

16. For descriptions of the models see pp. 6–7, above. Comparison of the short-term effects of all of the programs on achievement measures appears less and less

each of them, substantial prior research has been carried out. Each of the sponsors argues that use of its treatment should produce substantial short-term effects on certain standardized achievement tests, and each can point to a primitive theory and to considerable prior evidence to support its argument. Finally, each of these sponsors claims that the effects of its model should be evident on the achievement tests long after the treatment has ended though the argument for this claim is less persuasive than that for substantial short-term effects.

These treatments meet the conditions of explicit purpose, prior testing, and development and promise substantial, measurable effects in laboratory and small-scale experiments. For them, the large-scale field studies of planned variations are a useful test of the possibility of putting the treatments into operation in a large number of sites across the country. The variation of conditions at the selected sites should provide a rigorous test of the general effectiveness of the models.

Even with these conditions, however, determining whether the difference in effects at various sites is a product of the implementation of the model or of its extension to a variety of users is a potentially serious problem. But with adequate preparation, it should be soluble. A program could be applied, in a controlled experiment, to two or three samples from limited and carefully specified populations. The larger less-controlled field experiment could then include embedded studies of program effects on subjects identified as similar to those in the preliminary controlled experiment. Differences between effects on these subjects in the two experiments might then be attributed to problems of implementing a program in a large, weakly controlled field study. If such differences were small and yet differences in effects among various subgroups in the field study were still substantial, that would be evidence that the program was more appropriate for one subgroup than another.

Finally it should be realized that the process of implementing curriculum treatments may actually change the treatments, so that a laboratory curriculum would somehow differ intrinsically from an ostensibly similar field curriculum. If that is so, the only externally valid curricula would be those developed in a field setting—a setting something like the planned variations setting.

Few data exist to support or refute such an idea, and the results of the data that do exist are mixed. On the one hand, the findings of the

reasonable as the inappropriateness of the measurements and the theoretical inadequacies of the models become more apparent.

third cohort of Follow Through and the second cohort of Head Start Planned Variation suggest that structured-reinforcement models produce effects in the field similar to effects found in the laboratory. Since these are the only models that meet the criteria for a valid planned variation study, this suggests that effects found in the laboratory studies might be generalized in the field. On the other hand, data gathered by first-hand observation suggest that some teachers modify the packaged treatments to their own tastes once they are safely ensconced in their own class-rooms. Then once again the problem becomes one of understanding the nature of a program to determine what consequences changes in the field might have.

DAVID K. COHEN

# The Value of
# Social Experiments

Fashions in social research change with fair regularity. One recent fascination has been "policy-relevant research," a commodity that became popular in the mid-1960s. The idea seemed simple enough: if researchers would work as hard on the dilemmas facing decision makers as they did on the puzzles facing professors, policy would be more effective. Social scientists have used many words on this subject in the past ten years, and an even larger number of dollars have been spent by government agencies—several hundreds of millions, in fact.

The money went for projects ranging from evaluations of local Head Start centers to computer simulations of national policy problems. But the most highly regarded member of this new species of research rapidly became the social experiment. Policy-oriented research was chiefly concerned with the effects of deliberate social change, and the shortcomings of nonexperimental inquiry soon became painfully apparent. Studies of existing practice were limited because existing practice was limited; the programs of any given moment hardly exhausted possible programs. Evaluation of innovative programs seemed an attractive alternative, but experience revealed weaknesses there as well. Program managers cared little for such methodological niceties as control groups, for example, because they interfered with the services. As experience with surveys and evaluation accumulated, the more controlled conditions of experimentation seemed a more appealing way of gaining valid evidence about the effects of change.

Valid evidence is always sure to excite researchers, but in this case it enticed government agencies as well. Four major social experiments in education were launched in the late 1960s. Their annual budgets ranged from thirty or forty million dollars down to about five million dollars but all together their yearly bill was in the neighborhood of one hundred million dollars. In the modest world of social research, that is a very large sum.

The notion behind these costly ventures seemed straightforward. Research on schools and evaluations of educational innovations during the middle 1960s showed little differential effectiveness among schools or programs. This was stiff news, and there was enormous disagreement about the explanation. One line of thought was that the research was flawed and the schools fine. Another was that the studies were correct and the schools hopeless. Still another argument was that the schools were potentially productive, but simply not doing the right things. Still another view was that while some schools were doing the right things, they were not doing enough.[1] Nearly everyone could agree, however, that evidence to resolve this debate was not in hand. Unless schools tried to do just those things that were not being done—or done well, or done enough—and the results were carefully evaluated, one would never know whether schools could be more effective. Experiments seemed the most promising way to resolve the issue; many thought they would also demonstrate just how schools could improve.

The social experiments in education, then, sought both to answer questions about school effectiveness which have bedeviled U.S. social policy since the early 1960s, and to demonstrate some promising new approaches. One wonders whether they succeeded. Did they provide better evidence about school effects, or about the effectiveness of new educational approaches? Did they bring better evidence to bear on policy issues?

### The Lessons of the Experiments

The experiments best suited for answering those queries are Head Start Planned Variation (HSPV) and Follow Through. Both of these federally sponsored programs began late in the Great Society, amid the

---

1. This debate has raged for nearly a decade. For some representative views, see Frederick Mosteller and Daniel P. Moynihan (eds.), *On Equality of Educational Opportunity* (Random House, 1972); and *Equal Educational Opportunity,* a special issue of the *Harvard Educational Review,* vol. 38, no. 1 (1968).

clouds of doubt which had engulfed earlier hopes for social reform through education. Follow Through was sponsored by the U.S. Office of Education. It focused on primary school children (in kindergarten and the first three grades), and it began first. It set out to test a dozen or so promising approaches to better education for the disadvantaged. The innovations would be installed in a variety of local schools, so that researchers could later compare their impact on children with the effects of the educational program in control schools that had no innovations. Head Start Planned Variation (sponsored by the Office of Economic Opportunity), began a year or so later, but it applied the same design and the same innovative models in Head Start centers.

Evaluating these experiments was no mean task. Several of the nation's leading applied research firms assisted by many academic experts carried out the work. One result has been a mounting number of lengthy technical research reports. Another has been a much more modest pile of brief nontechnical summaries—for those unhappy with statistics or thick reports.

Conspicuously absent among all the results, though, is any resolution of the policy issues to which the experiments were addressed. There is no greater clarity about schools' effectiveness at the experiments' close than there was at their inception. In fact, Lois-ellin Datta, one of the federal officials chiefly responsible for the Head Start experiment, commented that the results were not very helpful:

Apparently HSPV has not yielded much new information that will be useful in improving national programs. Even if, in the final analysis, the three years' study shows few differences among sponsors, the validity of this conclusion as a basis for national policy will be open to question. The design as implemented may have so much "noise" that its sensitivity to differential effects is reduced seriously.[2]

Recent assessments of the experiments—many of them drawn together by the Brookings Institution in this set of conference papers—suggest the same conclusion. Neither experiment seems to have resolved the issues it was aimed at.

If anything, in fact, matters are more complicated now, partly as a direct result of the experiments. For while no old confusions seem to have been resolved, several new ones appeared en route. This pattern is most clear in discussions of the experiments' results—which begin

2. Remarks during April 1973 conference of the Brookings Panel on Social Experimentation.

with different interpretations of what the experiments reveal about school effectiveness. One school of thought holds that the Planned Variation results generally confirm other findings that differences in schools' educational resources have no considerable or consistent relation to differences in student achievement. On this view the experiments support research like the Coleman Report, which found only weak differences in schools' effectiveness.[3] The other school of thought is that when treatments were well specified and appropriate outcome measures were used, schools were differentially effective. On this view the experiments are thought to show that research in the Coleman tradition is flawed, because it used global outcome measures to assess unfocused treatments. When schooling and its outcomes are well defined, positive results appear.[4]

The support for these views, of course, is derived from the same experimental data—seen differently. For those of the gloomy persuasion, one important point is that in Head Start Planned Variation none of the models consistently did better than their comparisons—good results in one year did not repeat in the next. Secondly, in no cases did *all* experimental sites in a model clearly perform at higher levels than their comparisons. And third, no consistent pattern of differences in effectiveness emerged among the sponsored treatments. The evaluations show a few cases in which particular sponsors produced greater gains than others. But these gains were inconsistent across the tests used in the experiment. Sponsors that produced gains on one test in HSPV did not produce gains on others.

This pattern seems to carry over into Follow Through, though the analysis is not complete. Most of the sponsored treatments do not appear to consistently outperform each other or their comparison groups: sponsors that do well in one year do not seem to repeat this performance in the following year.

Observers of a more hopeful sort, by contrast, point to the fact that some sponsored treatments that had distinct aims, that were clearly related to specific outcome measures, and that tailored methods and materials to those outcomes did sometimes perform better than others. These models had structured classroom techniques and were focused chiefly on cognitive development. The leading examples are the Be-

3. See pp. 135–36, above.

4. Remarks of Lois-ellin Datta, David Weikart, and Garry L. McDaniels during April 1973 conference of the Brookings Panel on Social Experimentation.

havior Analysis, High/Scope, and Englemann-Becker curricula. And in several sites on some tests these did produce higher scores than comparison sites.

One response to these optimistic claims has been that several of the sponsored treatments thought to have done well in Follow Through (Behavior Analysis and Englemann-Becker) did not do particularly well in Head Start. This is puzzling, since the models are the same in both experiments. In addition, one model (High/Scope) which did astonishingly well in one Follow Through site on one test (the Stanford-Binet), registered no such gains in the Head Start experiment on three of four tests. And it showed only small gains on the other instrument. Finally, the three programs that are thought to have succeeded because of their structured focus on cognition did not seem to affect the same outcome measures. When High/Scope sites in Follow Through showed gains, they were chiefly on the Stanford-Binet and not the Metropolitan Achievement Test, but this was reversed for the other two structured sponsors. The Behavior Analysis and Englemann-Becker sites did not perform well on the only Head Start test (Book 4A on the NYU) on which High/Scope made even a modest positive showing.[5]

In effect, then, two contrary arguments have been advanced to explain the same set of results. This disagreement has produced an additional cloud of explanations and arguments, in an effort to account both for the results and the disagreement. Some analysts ascribe the confusion to statistical problems in the data and analysis—and they despair of any resolution. By contrast, sponsors of unstructured models claim that the negative results occur because none of the tests were really appropriate. They think that the impact will only show up much later in children's school careers, and perhaps not on cognitive tests.[6] Other sponsors think that they had a real cognitive effect in the schoolroom, but claim that existing tests were largely insensitive to it. They argue that different cognitive tests are needed.[7] Sponsors of unstructured models also claim that their approaches were more difficult to implement than behaviorist models, because they require more complicated learning and broader engagement from teachers. They argue that the

5. Marshall S. Smith, *Some Short Term Effects of Project Head Start: A Report on the Second Year of Planned Variation—1970–71* (Cambridge, Mass.: Huron Institute, 1973), pp. 8 and 51–53.

6. Anne Monaghan, Huron Institute, in interviews with Bank Street College of Education sponsors of Head Start Planned Variation model.

7. Remarks of Weikart during April 1973 conference.

experiments ended just when their more complex models were reaching decent performance levels.[8]

These arguments are interesting and useful. But one point clearly is that the experiments' major question—can schools' differential effectiveness be improved—seems no nearer an answer now than it was in 1967. The better part of a decade's work and tens of millions of dollars have produced more arguments than answers. A second point concerns the arguments. Not only are there radically different interpretations of the experimental results, but there are contrary explanations of why the differing interpretations occur. There are arguments about the arguments. But these cannot be resolved empirically at present because they all refer to evidence that does not exist. They turn on notions about what a really appropriate test would be or how long implementation actually takes for various models, or on the measurement of things presently unmeasurable.

In fact, the experiments have not only produced new evidence that further complicates old issues; they also have created new issues. Or at least they have brought to center stage problems formerly buried deep in the wings. The best example of this is the tests. When the experiments began, all sponsors agreed to standardized tests as the criteria for measuring impact—though one said they paid little attention to the issue.[9] By the time the experiments drew to a close, though, many sponsors and researchers rejected this view, and seriously questioned the tests' appropriateness. This was partly because of the gloomy results the tests kept revealing, and partly because experience with implementing the new programs raised questions not apparent to sponsors at the outset. But either way, the experiments helped open up an issue that had long seemed settled; by 1972, attacking old tests or devising new ones had become a popular pastime.

If this describes the experiments' disappointing performance, it hardly explains it. One wants to know why things turned out as they did. The investment of hope and money, after all, was great, and besides, the story may reflect on other efforts to produce policy-relevant evidence.

### Explaining the Results

The experiments were complex social undertakings, so there are reasons sufficient to every taste. One reason concerns the tension be-

8. Ibid.
9. Ibid.

tween service and learning. The planned variation efforts tried to produce rigorous evidence about educational alternatives by imposing experimental frameworks on operating school agencies. But the logical requirements of experimentation were not always congruent with the operating requirements of schools. In the ensuing conflicts, experimental learning suffered. A second point concerns the uncertain nature of knowledge in education. The models generally had a weak basis in theory and research and it was therefore ordinarily impossible to know exactly the best way to implement them, or to know when they were well implemented, or to predict specifically what their effects would be. There simply were no clear standards or guides to action in either theory or the past experience of sponsors. As a result, while the experiments produced enormous quantities of evidence, its meaning remained unclear. In fact, because there was no settled intellectual interpretive context, more evidence produced more complexity.

A third point concerns learning in action. Because social policy consists largely of efforts to deal with hitherto unsolved social problems, it often is a collective venture into the unknown. As a result, the logic of learning about social problem-solving tends not to be what is expected in more settled fields of knowledge application. Instead of moving from stable research and theory to trials and thence to new practices, knowledge in social policy generally moves from action to understanding, from relatively untried programs and projects to frequently surprising evidence about their results.

These three points bear exploration, because they connect the lack of policy-relevant evidence in the experiments to broader patterns of relation between applied social research and social policy.

### Service and Learning

Social experiments straddle a dilemma. In principle, an experiment represents one of the most self-conscious and purposive systems for learning yet devised. Unlike everyday events, a good experiment is a model of intentional structure: what one wants to know is clearly defined; all relevant action is deliberate; and extraneous influences are screened out. A good experiment therefore produces much more precise, internally valid, and generalizable knowledge than studies of naturally occurring events.

But social experiments seek to illuminate alternative ways of defining or delivering social services, and this is neither a simple nor a neutral activity. Both providers and recipients of social services almost always have strong views about them, and they typically care more about the goods to be delivered than about some hypothetical scheme for other goods, alternate delivery, or greater efficiency. As a result, it is difficult to make social service systems and subjects accept experimental manipulation. In the planned variation experiments, for example, many minority-group members regarded some of the sponsored treatments with hostility or suspicion. They believed that the experiments' purpose was to decide what sort of education was good for their children. They were dubious about the criteria that might be used to make this determination and they wondered whether any criterion but one accepted by the people affected was relevant. In effect, they viewed the sponsored treatments as political choices, rather than as scientific ways to improve understanding of the learning process.

Of course, the treatments were both things at once. Social experiments represent efforts to marry intentional learning to political change. They do not occur in the carefully circumscribed world of formal inquiry, but in the midst of struggles over public values and resources. And because they seek to impose the logic of formal inquiry on the unruly world of social policy, social experiments experience serious internal tensions, between the logic of learning and the demands of action. These tensions tend to undermine the strength of inferences from experiments; in the planned variation cases this was true on a massive scale.

GENERALIZING RESULTS. One central concern in experimental thought is that results can be generalized to the entire relevant population. The chief device for achieving this has been random assignment of subjects to experimental and control conditions. Random assignment prevents any confusion between a treatment's real effects and results that might appear if subjects were selected on some special criteria, or if they were allowed to select themselves. The underlying idea, of course, is that experimental treatments are uniformly interesting to and applicable across entire populations.

In spite of this, various forms of selectivity affected decisions about participation in the education experiments. Districts, schools, and Head Start centers could decline to participate if they so desired; sometimes they joined by invitation, or by initiating efforts to participate; and often the "better" schools or centers were nominated to participate by school districts or regional OEO offices—precisely because they were better. Similar considerations also affected decisions about the assignment of schools and centers to experimental and control conditions.[10] Randomization was not used.

The underlying reasons for this result, of course, are that voluntarism was and is a major American political tradition, and decentralization a central fact of U.S. political life—especially in education. Assigning different varieties of corn to experimental plots is not a political problem. But random assignment of teachers to curricula or children to schools would have departed quite sharply from established political practice. It would have been not simply a device to enhance experimental learning, but a political innovation.

Without the benefit of randomization, analyses of the data have tried to compensate for selection biases, but one never knows whether the tactics have been successful. This is because the possible biases are not entirely known. As a result, it is unclear how far the experimental results apply, or for whom they are valid. This has created understandable problems in making inferences from the results, and it has generated some discussion about random assignment. There may be situations—more modest and manageable than these two massive efforts—in which random assignment is plausible. And it may be more sensible to think of generalizing to populations already willing to try a particular innovation. For any given experiment, a pool of willing volunteers could be recruited on the basis of interest, and then randomly assigned to treatment and control conditions. Random assignment could thus be preserved within the constraints of voluntarism.

The second suggestion transforms selectivity from a problem into a solution—simply by agreeing to generalize results only to those committed to a given innovation. If such efforts worked, they would in some sense solve the problem of external validity. But they would also produce greater uncertainty about inferences from experiments, because of the difficulty of defining a population whose limiting attribute is commitment to one specific treatment. Such a population would vary in unknown

10. In the case of Head Start Planned Variation, for example, management of the experiment was closely related to the management of the program. Experimental centers were not chosen randomly as a result. Instead, the program managers sometimes seem to have nominated their best centers to participate in the experiment. David K. Cohen, "Politics and Research: The Evaluation of Social Action Programs in Education," *Review of Educational Research,* vol. 40 (April 1970), p. 228; Carol Lukas, "Social Experimentation: the Case of Head Start Planned Variation" (Harvard Graduate School of Education, 1973; processed), p. 28; Richard F. Elmore, "The Politics and Administration of an Educational Experiment" (Harvard Graduate School of Education, 1973; processed), pp. 34–35.

ways with particular innovations—presumably different sorts of schools would be interested in open classrooms than in the Englemann-Becker curriculum. It would be difficult to know in advance exactly for whom experimental inferences held in any given case.

This problem would be exacerbated by the fact that over a period of time experimental findings would doubtless affect this population characteristic: experiments that failed to produce positive effects would usually have a smaller and less enthusiastic audience than those that succeeded. As a result, limiting generalizability on the basis of interest or commitment would not clarify the applicability of findings.

The seriousness of this problem very much depends on who the audience for experimental results is imagined to be. If it were central administrators or social scientists who desire predictive knowledge about the impact of given treatments on known populations, the problem would be serious indeed. Thinking this was the critical audience would make sense either in a society that enshrined social science, or in one in which most decisions were taken centrally and obeyed locally. The United States, of course, is neither. But if the audience is potential adopters of innovations in local schools and school districts, they have little need to make predictions about the impact of treatments on broad population groups. Their chief concern will be the impact of a given innovation for them. The audience consists of one, and evidence about commitment to an innovation would be self-knowledge alone. Thinking that local adopters were the critical audience makes sense if many decisions about innovations are made locally—as they are in the United States.

Thus, the applicability of the experiments' findings was rendered uncertain by selection of schools to the experiment, to particular treatments, and to experimental or control groups. The experiments' managers judged this selectivity to be necessary for political and social reasons—the experiment, they reasoned, could not survive unless it conformed to prevailing ideas about political choice. In the conflict between norms for services and rules for experimental procedure, the social service norms therefore prevailed. Knowledge about the generality of the experimental results was limited, and policy inferences from the evidence were necessarily weak.

VALID EFFECTS. If selectivity presented obstacles to generalizing results, it also muddied the question of whether the experimental treatments had any effects. In Follow Through, for example, many of the schools that received a particular curriculum seem to have had prior experience with it, or something similar; but the control schools usually had not. As a result, it is possible that familiarity with the experimental curriculum could have caused treatment effects.

This result is to be expected, because education agencies provide social services; they care less about experimental than service goals. Evidence from the two planned variation efforts and other experiments suggests that centers or schools that volunteered for particular treatments were motivated by an interest in the innovation—and often by some acquaintance with it, or even partial prior implementation of it—not by an abstract commitment to experimentalism. The volunteers in such situations wanted to further explore a known quantity, or to get more support for an innovation already under way, or both. In the planned variation experiments there were many symptoms of such problems. There was spontaneous diffusion of treatments from experiments to controls in local sites; there also were deliberate efforts on the part of local program managers to apply the innovation to control as well as experimental subjects, in order to avoid unfairness; there also was difficulty in securing control populations.[11]

Thus, there are pressures in social service systems against segregating attractive resources in arbitrarily selected populations. These lead both to self-selection to treatments and to spreading treatment resources beyond the treatment groups. It would be difficult to deal with these problems in any social setting, but the difficulties are magnified in education. The schools are a decentralized system; the society is committed to voluntary action and endlessly fascinated by innovation; and the public expects education to be universally and equally provided.

The most striking point, though, is the tension between the need for commitment in mounting experimental innovations, and the need for impartiality in experimental trials. Experimenters always want to know whether the effects of an innovation are due to the treatment or to the special commitment, expertise, or experience of the experimental subjects. Some commentators have noticed this problem and suggested incentives for participation as controls, to lessen the effects of selectivity in attractive treatments. Another suggestion has been to assign subjects

---

11. See Smith, *Some Short Term Effects,* pp. 8 and 51–53. See also Anne Monaghan, Carol Lukas, and David Cohen, *Follow-up Study on HSPV* (Huron Institute, forthcoming), chapter on Bank Street, Site A, for example.

to experimental and control conditions randomly from a pool of committed volunteers.

There is, however, something troublesome in these ideas. Innovators want and need understanding and commitment on the part of participants in an experiment. Education, like other social services, involves more than the exercise of neutral professional expertise—the educator's values cannot be held in abeyance. Education is a political and moral endeavor, characterized in almost every aspect by competing moral, political, and esthetic ideas. Neutrality in matters concerning the style, substance, and organization of schooling is quite foreign to the enterprise. The service system in which experiments occur demands the very commitment that erodes experimental impartiality. For any innovator, a "fair" test of his idea requires teachers who are committed, principals who are supportive, school systems that want the product, and so on. But for the experimenter, a fair test is one in which the participants in treatment and control programs differ not at all in respect to commitment, prior experience, and the like.

Thus, the two notions of fairness are at cross purposes. There is no simple way to resolve the tension, because the demands of impartial knowledge are no less reasonable than the partiality required to produce social innovation. But if selectivity owing to commitment cannot be eliminated from many experimental situations, selection should not be regarded as a source of internal invalidity. Partiality and selection would be valid requirements of innovation or social action. Randomization to avoid selection would not be indicated.

In these circumstances, the measurement of experimental effects might focus instead on historical approaches—assessing the impact of social innovations by comparing them to some preexisting conditions. Shifting to such an approach would eliminate some problems in attributing effects to treatments, but it would create others. When the reference point for judging effects is a preexisting condition rather than a control group, the chances of undetected confounding between the effects of treatments and other changes in subjects (such as normal maturation) is considerable. There is no independent standard of comparison—no otherwise equal untreated group of subjects. Moreover, historical changes often occur in experimental treatments. There is, for example, evidence of both sponsor-induced and externally caused changes in the planned variation treatments. This squares with other research on innovations in education, which suggests that innovations are weakly specified and undergo major changes during implementation.[12] Of course, this threat to internal validity arising from developmental instability would exist within a classically experimental framework as well. An historical approach simply highlights the problem.

There are, then, competing conceptions of valid knowledge about the effects of innovations: selectivity and commitment on the part of experimental subjects seems essential from the perspective of innovators and operating agencies, but it weakens inference in classical designs. Once again, the issue can be reduced to a matter of audiences. If the audience for experimental results is the potential local user, then selectivity is no problem, because members of this audience would adopt the innovation only if committed. As a result the possible confounding of selection and treatment effects is a nonissue. But if the audience consists of central administrators (or social scientists) concerned with general policy and the cost-effectiveness of social programs, then the potential confounding appears fatal, because identifying the costs and benefits of treatments, and separating them from "natural" influences seems essential to sound central policy advice. This tension was sometimes recognized but never resolved in the planned variation experiments.

### Uncertain Knowledge

A second reason for the limited policy relevance of the experimental results is the absence of clear standards of success. In most cases the treatments' outcomes were not well specified; it was not clear what a successful result would be; nor could it be known when a treatment was properly implemented. This peculiar situation was not primarily the consequence of sponsors' oversight or poor planning, but the result of weak knowledge about education. Research and theory in this field provide imprecise guidance for educational practice, and uncertain criteria for evaluating action. Because of this, the lessons of experience are often in doubt.

12. See Neal C. Gross, Joseph B. Giacquinta, and Marilyn Bernstein, *Implementing Organizational Innovations: A Sociological Analysis of Planned Educational Change* (Basic Books, 1971); W. W. Charters, Jr., and others, *The Process of Planned Change in the School's Instructional Organization* (University of Oregon, Center for the Advanced Study of Educational Administration, 1973); Seymour Sarason, *The Culture of the School and the Problem of Change* (Allyn and Bacon, 1971); Louis M. Smith and Patricia M. Keith, *Anatomy of Educational Innovation: An Organizational Analysis of an Elementary School* (Wiley, 1971).

IMPLEMENTATION. Information about the degree to which experimental treatments were actually implemented was essential, because it might help to explain outcome differences among sites. It could be, for example, that schools scoring poorly on tests did so because they had only partially installed their model. While many participants in the planned variation efforts subscribed to this notion, evaluation reports suggest that no one has enough evidence to either prove or refute it.[13]

This result did not occur for want of trying. Data on implementation were collected, but were not particularly informative. The rather naive notion was that what was needed was a quick check, simply to find out if treatments had been installed or not. Implementation studies were thus conceived as checklists to be filled out by teachers, sponsors, or their consultants. In all cases the purpose was to indicate whether a treatment was implemented or not.[14]

The evaluation contractor and the sponsors dutifully devised the brief paper and pencil checklists, and collected evidence on scores of classrooms. Evaluators then analyzed the resulting data, and duly discovered that they could not interpret what "well-implemented" on these lists actually meant. They did not know whether the several raters used the same criteria for assessing implementation. And they could not decide why there were year-to-year differences in ratings for the same sites, or what they signified.[15] The problem, of course, was that the data had been collected on the simplistic assumptions that participants and evaluators knew what a fully implemented model looked like, that they could agree on this point, and that installation of the experimental treatments was a mechanical matter, which could be checked on in simple and straightforward lists. But the evidence collected showed that this was not so. In response the experiments' administrators set on foot several more sophisticated observational studies of implementation.[16] The researchers directing these efforts quite naturally turned first to the sponsors to specify the characteristics and relative importance of the elements in the models, so they would have a correct basis for making overall judgments about implementation. But the researchers found less clarity on these points than they had hoped. Sponsors often had difficulty identifying

13. See pp. 115–18, above.
14. Ibid.
15. Ibid.
16. One of these studies was Monaghan, Lukas, and Cohen, *Follow-up Study;* another, set under way for Follow Through by a consulting firm in Oregon, is as yet incomplete.

and sorting out the elements in their models. This was partly due to disinterest—sponsors often were concerned less with analysis than action. In part it was due to differences between practitioners and researchers: researchers sought neat categories, but sponsors viewed their models holistically. Finally, it was difficult to specify elements because they changed: a sponsor's conception of his model during the experiment's third year was often different from his conception in the first year.[17]

If a sponsor could not define the model, how could a researcher decide if it was properly implemented? In assessing the relative importance of elements within each model, sponsors were asked to explain which parts of their innovation were more important than others. Some sponsors said flatly that they could not do it. Others tried, but were uncertain about the validity of their judgments. Still others could name a few elements that seemed most important, but could go no further. Several observed that their ideas about the relative importance of elements had changed as a result of experience—and they opined that change might occur again.[18]

When observers actually visited the schools and Head Start centers, they found that the models were more complex in practice than they had seemed on paper, or in interviews with sponsors. Sites often had different interpretations of the models than sponsors had—and some of them made good sense to the observers. This put a fine edge on questions about whose standard of implementation ought to prevail. The ensuing research reports concluded that it was not clear what a properly implemented model was. Even the best observational research, they pointed out, could not make up for cloudiness in the conception of treatments, changes in definition due to practical experience, and diverse criteria of implementation.

This is only to be expected. The planned variation models, like most innovations in education, arose primarily from practice—they were not deduced from theory, nor constructed inferentially from research. More precise knowledge, which would have permitted more precise standards for gauging and interpreting implementation, simply did not exist. Not being able to measure implementation very well meant that no one could be sure whether, or how much, the intended experiments had actually occurred. This made it harder, in turn, to interpret test score outcomes. Did the experiments prove that the treatments were ineffective? Or did

17. Monaghan interviews.
18. Ibid.

they prove that most treatments were not well implemented? Because knowledge about the innovations was weak and research on implementation was poor, these questions went begging. The chief lesson is that if such experiments are ever undertaken again, much more attention ought to be given to implementation. While this is a good lesson and true, it does not help policymakers to wring helpful morals from these recent ventures in policy research.

OUTCOMES. A second example of the problem of uncertain knowledge occurs in the case of experimental effects. When the planned variation experiments began, the principal question was whether some treatments would boost achievement test scores more than others. The tests used to measure IQ and achievement had been used to assess various school programs for more than four decades. Their appropriateness as criteria of school effectiveness was not in doubt; it was widely believed that tests measured what schools sought to accomplish.

Soon after the experiments began, though, this conviction started to erode. Preliminary evidence repeated the same depressing pattern of other recent school program evaluations: the children in special programs seemed to do no better than those in regular school programs. Some persons reacted to these deliveries of bad news by attacking the messengers: researchers, they argued, were biased and purveying racist ideas. Others attacked the programs: too little and too late, they said.[19]

Still others took aim at the tests, and these questions turned out to be central. One line of attack focused on cultural content: the tests embodied middle-class white culture, it was argued, and were therefore unfair to minorities and the poor.[20] Another focused on the match between programs and outcomes: schools really did not do what the tests assumed, because (especially in the slums) schools did little more than babysit or try to maintain order. But by far the most important question was whether the tests were at all suitable for assessing the average effect of programs on groups of subjects. Several researchers pointed out that the tests, after all, had been specifically designed to measure differences

19. These arguments have been advanced more often in newspapers than academic journals, but they were more or less summarized in the *Harvard Educational Review's* May 1973 issue (vol. 43) devoted to reviews of Christopher S. Jencks and others, *Inequality: A Reassessment of the Effect of Family and Schooling in America* (Basic Books, 1972).

20. These arguments were summarized in various essays devoted to the Jensen controversy, published in *Harvard Educational Review*, vol. 41 (May 1971).

among individuals.[21] Items are included in tests only when they differentiate well among individuals, and tend to be rejected when they differentiate among curricula, or sexes, or regions, or school programs. This is due partly to psychologists' affinity for normally distributed results (which group differences would undermine), and partly to test publishers' affinity for products that will sell in many school systems (which use many different curricula). The researchers evaluating the new education programs began to argue that existing tests of reading measure individual differences in general linguistic and conceptual ability within the mainstream culture, but do not assess attainment within a particular curriculum or school program. The tests are designed precisely to screen out group and curriculum differences; for that reason they might not accurately reflect differences in the effectiveness of various innovative curricula.

This notion sent psychometricians diving back into their item pools, to devise new tests that were referenced specifically to particular curriculum objectives or learning criteria. Their hope was that such tests would measure specific school achievement rather than general abilities, and would therefore measure the effectiveness of particular school programs more accurately. The new tests may or may not do this.

Thus fundamental doubts about existing social program evaluation results were raised and persist. Negative evaluation results may have less to do with the schools than with the measures of impact. Evidence to decide this issue is not available, but the questions have affected thought and research. In fact, the issue has changed: Is the problem one of schools' ineffectiveness, or one of tests' insensitivity?

Another general assumption at the experiments' inception was that tests were important because they measured the skills needed to succeed in adult life. Test scores were taken as a measure of such skills, and therefore as a reliable predictor of students' later social and economic destinations. These venerable ideas had permeated educational thought and practice for decades prior to the 1960s, and there was no reason the Great Society should have been an exception.

Once again, though, when negative evaluation results began to filter in, some researchers wondered just exactly what tests did stand for. Especially in view of the Coleman Report's findings that schools were

21. George F. Madaus, "Memorandum to the Joint Committee [of American Society for Measurement and Evaluation] on *Test Standards Revision*," May 7, 1973.

not differentially effective, it seemed reasonable to look again at basic assumptions about how schools affected performance later in life.

The results of this work were similar to the testing research discussed just above. Some investigators found, for example, that IQ or achievement test scores apparently had no independent impact on occupational status or income: among men with the same level of education, those with higher test scores did not systematically earn more money or wind up in higher status jobs. Other researchers found that among workers in the same occupational groups, earlier test scores were unrelated either to job performance, productivity, or supervisors' ratings of work.[22] These and other findings began to suggest that whatever tests did measure, it might not be the skills required to succeed economically in America.

By the time the planned variation results were being written, therefore, the evaluators felt constrained to say that while the reports were mostly concerned with test scores, they were not exactly sure what the tests did measure, nor confident that they measured attributes important to children's lives or later success. The outcome criteria which had seemed so solid and self-evident at the outset had lost much of their legitimacy by the conclusion. As a result, the policy question that had been at the experiments' center in 1968—are school programs differentially effective in raising test scores?—dissolved into several other, more fundamental questions by 1972. One was whether tests were a fair measure of what schools did; another was whether what schools did— or tests measured—were at all related to how adults performed; still another was how educational change occurred, and why implementation was so variable and difficult. Lacking firm criteria for evaluating implementation or impact, it was difficult to derive policy advice from the evaluations. In fact, due to the absence of solid criteria for success or failure, the experiments generated a host of issues about how success might be defined and measured. As a result, while advice flows from the experiments, it has more to do with research and evaluation than policy.

It is worth asking why this happened. Why were standards of success in implementation and impact so hard to come by? One reason was that the experiments were not set under way chiefly to advance knowledge about the effects of schooling. They were designed mainly to improve programs for disadvantaged children. Thus, the treatments were defined by casting about for promising educational practices, not by consulting

22. Jencks and others, *Inequality,* chap. 7.

theory and research to make sure that the right questions about the effects of schooling were asked.

This is an entirely reasonable and predictable feature of knowledge accumulation in a social service. The experiments, like most educational innovations, occurred because of problems and opportunities presented by practice. Social experimentation is not a process with its own pure cognitive logic, but an outgrowth of educational practice and social policymaking—which have a different logic. The "questions" the experiments were supposed to answer therefore were problems of service provision—in this case deficiencies in education for the disadvantaged—not problems defined by theory or empirical research.

This helps to explain why existing definitions of school outcomes were accepted with little or no hesitation: the point of the experiments was more to improve schools' performance than to raise questions about why schools did or did not perform. Since the definition of the problem— the schools' "failure"—rested on evidence about low test scores, it seemed natural to define success in terms of higher test scores. And in fact, when opposition to the test arose later on, it stemmed from practical concerns—the sponsors' resistance to blanket impact evaluation, and social anguish about negative program results—not from theoretically inspired questions about the schooling process. Both questions and answers in the experiments arose in a disorderly cloud, like dust from an old rug. The two ventures had not been conceived or designed to pursue research issues, so when basic puzzles appeared, the evaluations had not been devised to help decide them.[23] Although lessons are being learned from the experiments, they are mostly independent of the experiments' design or the experimenters' intentions. And they are more relevant to research than to policy.

A second reason why clear standards of success were lacking is related to the structure of theory in education. Several treatments had a self-conscious relation to scientific theory: the High/Scope program for example, was based on Piagetian ideas of development; the Behavior Analysis program is related to behavior modification conceptions of learning. The treatments, however, were not tests of theoretical ideas, but applications of them. They were not arranged to find out whether one theory of development offered a more satisfying explanation of developmental phenomena than some other theory, but to find out

---

23. This view was expressed by Marian S. Stearns at the April 1973 conference of the Brookings Panel on Social Experimentation.

whether particular developmental approaches "worked." This was due in part to the fact that the experiments were efforts to demonstrate improvements in a social service, and demonstrations encourage applications, not tests, of theories. But it also owes something to the character of education theory itself. It would not be easy to test the relative explanatory power of Piagetian and operant-conditioning theory, because while they both concern learning, they define the process and the phenomena quite differently—they involve different paradigms.[24] Copernican and ptolemaic theories of planetary motion agreed upon a body of phenomena to be explained, but disagreed on the explanation. In education—and other fields of social practice as well—there is no large common body of phenomena to be explained, because in such fields theories define the evidence as well as the explanation differently.

This makes it difficult to determine grounds for choosing among theories, and concentrates research work within theoretical traditions. Evidence that each theory is "true"—that is, accounts for some of the appearances—has discouraged efforts to find out if some theories are more true than others. Theoretical generality is sacrificed to theoretical plurality. A demonstration approach to research and experimentation is thereby encouraged. Creating experiments that pit conceptions against each other is relatively foreign to the pluralistic theoretical world of education, and research thus explores whether a given theory works at all. Any theory that works has roughly the same epistemological status as all the others that work. The reasons for choosing among them thus tend to be nonempirical.

For these reasons, then, experimentation occurs in an intellectual environment marked by diverse, competing, and noncomparable theoretical traditions. Consequently there is only weak guidance for inquiry: it is difficult to decide when treatments have been either implemented or successful, for there are no solid theoretical or empirical anchors for measures of either.

*Research and Action*

The notion that experimental results should inform policy is appealing. In principle, nothing is more sensible than trying out educational

---

24. Thomas S. Kuhn, *The Structure of Scientific Revolutions* (2nd ed., University of Chicago Press, 1970).

changes, recording the results, and then applying them to policy issues. But this appealing idea contains two assumptions that turned out to be fatal in practice. One is that social concerns will remain relatively stable over time, so that when experimental findings finally appear they will bear on still-vital policy problems. The other is that experimental issues as defined at the outset will seem correctly drawn at the experiment's end.

In the planned variation experiments, neither assumption seemed to hold. The experimental issues, for example, underwent rapid change during the endeavor. At the outset, the chief issue in both experiments was the impact of innovative curricula on test scores—an issue chosen in the hope that the performance of such curricula would help refute the negative conclusions concerning Great Society education programs that were being drawn from their initial evaluations and from the Coleman Report. While the experiments got slowly under way, however, the related social programs ground on, negative evaluations continued to pour out, and additional skeptical research on school effects (which had been stimulated by the Coleman Report) was published. Before the experiments were even half over, therefore, the research climate began to change. Published research continued to challenge the belief that better schooling would reduce poverty; and researchers also began to wonder what tests were, what scores on them meant, and whether test scores in school were related to adult economic or social performance. The longer the experiments continued the more doubts were raised about their premises, and the more it seemed that other issues, discovered along the way, were more fundamental.

This pattern of shifting issues reflected the relative weakness of knowledge concerning human development and the schooling process. But the process itself—the way research issues were generated and replaced—is informative. Because social action typically occurs in areas of weak knowledge, the results of interventions generally cannot be well predicted. Outcomes are often unexpected, and frequently at cross-purposes with program assumptions. This tends to corrode the ideas underlying programs and to generate new research questions.

There was similar instability in the social issues surrounding the experiments. When Follow Through began, it was expected that if the experiments successfully identified and demonstrated sound alternatives, policy would follow suit. One hope was that Follow Through—whose budget hopes had been an early domestic casualty of the Vietnam war—would be shifted from small-scale experimental status to its originally intended large-scale action status. Another was that extra moneys would be appropriated for Title I of the 1965 Elementary and Secondary Education Act to support promising new approaches. But these hopes all proved sterile. Shifting social moods and political opinion reduced interest in social action, and skeptical research raised questions about the value of investing in education. By 1973, therefore, there was not much of a federal market for positive experimental results in education, even if the experiments had produced them.

Priorities had shifted at the local level as well. Community groups and national organizations which had pressed for compensatory programs in the mid-1960s had begun to reconsider their position, as a result of growing interest in decentralization and community control. The notion that school failure arose from insufficient resources was being replaced by a new diagnosis—that school failure was the consequence of indifferent teachers, insensitive administrators, and politically unresponsive central boards. As a result, the remedies contemplated in compensatory programs began to seem questionable, if not downright ill-intentioned. And the local energy and interest that thus might have coalesced around successful experimental results became progressively less likely as sentiment shifted toward new policy directions.

In the space of less than ten years, then, the policy climate had shifted dramatically. Interest in remedies embodied in the experiments had diminished; the resources required to support new initiatives had also vanished; and new problem diagnoses and new ideas about remedy had become popular. The experiments were exploring policy options that were no longer entirely vital or viable. Cycles of reform in U.S. education—and in social policy generally—are often short and generally unpredictable. By the time experimental trials conclude, attention often shifts, or problems may be redefined. The lessons may therefore fall on deaf ears.

### Conclusion

One point in telling this story is simply to offer an interpretation for a more or less widely accepted fact: these two major ventures in policy research were a disappointment. The planned variation experiments did not produce the expected policy-relevant results, for several reasons. The nature of social services tends to defeat experimental learning. The character of knowledge in education makes it difficult to devise solid measures of success or failure. And learning about social policy generally seems to involve a movement from practice to theory—a backward progression from what appear to be self-evident ideas about social problems and remedies, through perplexing program results, to ever more fundamental inquiries about program assumptions and society. The result was that the knowledge resulting from the experiments tended to increase complexity rather than clarifying action alternatives. The experiments multiplied questions instead of producing answers.

The other point of the story concerns its implications for policy research more broadly. This is a more difficult matter, for these experiments are not the best examples of their species, and there are many varieties of policy research besides experimentation. Nonetheless, one modest observation might be in order. Reviewing applied researchers' criticism of nonexperimental policy research, one finds several persistent themes: that social interventions are vaguely conceived and weakly specified; that it is hard to tell whether, or how well they are implemented; that criterion measures are generally of dubious relevance or solidity; that evidence about the effects of such interventions is typically so uncertain that its value for policy is nil.

All of these arguments have been advanced as reasons why experimental research on social policy ought to be carried out: such research, it has been argued, would be much less likely to repeat the sins of nonexperimental inquiry. But the evidence suggests that these problems are as central in the experiments as anywhere else: in education, at least, experimentation did not appreciably reduce these problems. Social experiments simply provided a somewhat different setting in which familiar problems recurred—with roughly the same results. This need not be a discouragement to doing policy research, but it might be a caution against thinking that one or another method of research will ease the problems of learning from social action.

## Comment by Frederick Mosteller

The planned variation studies in Follow Through and Head Start cannot be called "controlled field studies"—that is, studies providing a direct comparison between educational models for which treatment and control groups have been randomly selected. Instead, these efforts are pilot studies of models forced into substantial use. Their merit lies in their exposing the difficulties of implementing educational programs. The implementation at a site of a given model demands both serious effort and considerable time to develop. Furthermore, these studies identify clearly the problems in specifying the model, even though they do not entirely solve the problems.

The plan in Figure 1, page 74, above, for developing a planned variation experiment goes a long way toward a realistic solution of some of the problems. Perhaps not as many as eleven years, nor as much as $6 billion, are needed to develop a model. Nevertheless, the idea of steady development, winding up with the controlled field trials, fits extremely well with efforts of this kind in other fields. It is encouraging that plans for such orderly development have been laid out by those sponsoring a particular model.

In an experiment including ten planned variation pilot studies, one of them should stand out as far as 1.5 standard deviations, on the average, by chance alone. The observed gains in the program that look best should be considerably larger; such gains, however, are evidently extremely rare, either across the board or for specific efforts. The wise policy to follow in planned variation studies would be to choose the best-looking programs and test them thoroughly.

Often a multiplicity of goals raises problems in comparing various program models, especially when each model has several goals. In the end, society should decide what it wants, not the researchers, not the teachers, and not even a panel of experts, though all these groups may advise.

Consequently it is necessary to weigh all of the variables that the various models are especially interested in promoting. The progress of each of the models or each of the variables should be measured at successive intervals of time. A variable such as consumer satisfaction might even be included for each model. If that is one of the variables society cares about, then it should be routinely measured for every model.

Later, society must look at what happened to the several variables and notice what progress has been made in such areas as language, mathematics, self-concepts, skills, ability to deal with other people, or civil rights attitudes. After reviewing that whole set of measures, society will have to assign weights to each measure or assess them as a whole, even though different progress is being made in different models at different times and on different variables. This is routine evaluation practice in other areas of inquiry. The idea that different schools produce different products is not an upsetting or new idea. It may be necessary to ask, "If we are only allowed to have a certain number of schools, how many do we want of each kind?"

The search for especially effective methods of education will go on just as the search for improvement goes on in every field. And even when the process seems to be extraordinarily effective, it may still have to be tested. Table 1 is a capsule summary of recent surveys of some thirty field experiments. All of these studies have had the benefit of pilot work. Further, they have all had the benefit of whatever social, medical, or economic theory has been available. They have had preliminary observational studies of the kind that might be appropriate for planned variation. Where preliminary sample surveys were appropriate, they have been made. Each study has been finally brought up to the point of a controlled field study complete with randomized trials. If the preliminary work had been perfectly carried out, then every one of these social or medical innovations would automatically have been a great success. Some of them appear to have caused modest improvements, but when costs are considered, they may not pay their way; others may have been poorer than the standard, quite apart from the cost of the program. Thirteen of the innovations have not contributed anything on the average. One experiment and one phase of another proved to be substantially worse than the control or standard.

The field trials studied include some social innovations, such as at-

**Table 1. Effects of Field Experiment on Selected "Promising" Innovations**

| | Number of innovations affected | | | | |
|---|---|---|---|---|---|
| Study | Substantially worse | Worse | No change | Some improve-ment | Substantial improve-ment |
| Elinson[a] | 0 | 1 | 5 | 3 | 1 |
| Boruch and Mosteller[b] | 0 | 0 | 4 | 2 | 2 |
| Surgery[c] | 1½ | 3 | 4 | 1 | 1½ |
| Total | 1½ | 4 | 13 | 6 | 4½ |

a. Ten studies collected and analyzed by Jack Elinson and Cyrille Gell of the Columbia University School of Public Health. Effect of innovation judged by Frederick Mosteller.

b. Eight controlled field trials collected by Robert Boruch of Northwestern University and Frederick Mosteller—collected separately but reported together for convenience. Effect of innovation judged by Mosteller.

c. Eleven surgical experiments, collected by Bucknam McPeek, John P. Gilbert, and Frederick Mosteller, with the assistance of Jolin R. Nixon. Effect of innovation judged by Mosteller.

tempts to reduce the number of delinquents by identifying potential delinquents and providing them with a substantial social program, and introducing fortified rice into diets to reduce beriberi. The fortified rice experiment was one that caused substantial improvement, reducing beriberi by 67 percent; a new way of handling a perforated appendix reduced the number of infections by about 30 percent.

Over a rather substantial range of health and welfare reforms, about 15 percent appear actually to have produced substantial positive results. That is far from a perfect showing and well under 50 percent. And these are reforms that had the benefit of extensive preliminary consideration and planning. When finally tried out, almost all failed. If one in seven of these well-researched social reforms turn out to be innovations that have substantial positive effects, then, even when preliminary work on an innovation is most encouraging, the matter cannot be settled without a controlled field trial.

And where the experiments involve rare events that are difficult to measure, it is important to persist to the stage of controlled field studies. Only through persistent search is some fresh new idea or a fresh implementation of an old idea that will yield improvement likely to be found, because most innovations do not work very well. Once a promising improvement appears, genuine controlled field studies must be run, and the time and funds required to do the job right must be found.

Since very few controlled field trials have been undertaken, early ones may be poorly executed. They are likely to elicit the kind of constructive criticism that the planned variation experiments received.

One of the objections to field trials is to the kind of tests that experimental groups must endure. As long as there are sites willing to implement one of a pair of models, they can be randomly assigned. There seems to be no serious ethical problem in most of this work because children are nearly impervious to all of the educational treatments offered, and all are intended benignly. No one proposes to try a placebo experiment of no schooling at all. In education, the ethical problem should be oriented toward the taxpayer: "Are we finding out the most we can for his dollar?" In the end, careful and firm work will do the most in that direction.

## Comment by James Coleman

The federal government has been initiating experiments and other research activities with schools for almost a decade. What is most noticeable is that schools have gotten worse during this period. For example, attendance rates have gone down precipitously in many cities, mostly among lower-class blacks, but in other social groups as well. Student scores on cognitive achievement tests have gone down in many cities, but probably not for that reason alone. There may not be a causal relation between the growth of federal attention and the decline of the schools, but, for a number of reasons, there may be.

If two equally qualified persons are trying to solve a general problem, one at a distance and the other locally, the latter will probably be more successful than the former. Most of the direction of the planned variation experiments is coming from persons who are trying to solve general problems at a distance. Yet local people are probably wiser in most particular cases. Their failure to apply that wisdom out of deference to knowledge gained in national studies constitutes a danger. The current state of knowledge about how schools affect children encourages a combination of deference and experiential wisdom at the local level. It may be that the ignorance rather than the wisdom gets applied.

The experimental paradigm adopted at the federal level appears to be wrong, or at least incomplete, for it assumes the existence of a single decision maker who requires some kind of information feedback. In schools, above all, there are a number of decision makers. One is the federal government, but it is the latest to enter and is probably the least important; another is administrators of the local school system; another is the local community that has to vote the taxes, bond issues, and so on to support the system; another is the parents of particular children; and still another is children themselves.

These decision makers are not all concerned solely about cognitive achievement. A number of outcomes are often more important to local school systems than grade-equivalent scores in reading achievement, and a number of outcomes are often more important to parents and children. Order in schools is probably of most importance to local school administrators. One of the major changes that has occurred in schools over the past five years has been a decline of order, but no one at the federal level has bothered to study that. Since 1965, federal agencies have been studying the effects of various treatments and surroundings on achievement, as measured by standardized test scores.

Attendance is also extremely important, to parents, children, and school administrators. Federal-level policy research has not bothered to focus on attendance at all.

Another possible effect of schools is the energy put into school activities by students. That is of some interest to parents; it is of some interest to students themselves; and it is even of some interest to schools. Pupil retention in schools is also extremely important from the point of view of administrators: How can children be kept in a school and their families kept from moving? The obverse of that is pupil happiness in the school, which is extremely important to the child.

These are all dependent variables, all outcomes of treatments that might be carried out in schools, outcomes that are of considerable importance to some educational decision makers. In addition, they are very much a function of the environment; they have no genetic component. Thus the school has an opportunity to influence them undeterred by genetic constraints.

Moreover, with these kinds of dependent variables, effects occur quickly, not over a long period of time. Some of these variables are necessary, though not sufficient, conditions for cognitive learning. In other words, if a student is not at school, or if he puts no energy into school activities, then he will learn little from a treatment given at school.

A practical reason for studying these outcomes is that something can be done about each of them: both politically and operationally they can be manipulated. There is less mystery about how to increase attendance, or interest in school, or teacher morale, than there is about how to create one year's increment in reading scores per school year.

In sum, these are not simply process variables, not just means to an end, but really important ends in themselves. Whatever treatments, whatever kind of planned variations, whatever kind of experimental activities are carried out, cognitive learning is probably not the most important dependent variable or outcome to be observed.

One extremely important dependent variable is the implementation of a program. Consider, as an example, "Sesame Street." Implementation in that case means something a little bit different than it does in Head

Start Planned Variation or Follow Through. It means whether the child views the program or not. But the original objective of research on "Sesame Street" was to determine the impact of "Sesame Street" on a child who was viewing the program. That is probably less important than the question, "What proportion of children—from various social classes and various ethnic and racial groups—will, on their own, watch 'Sesame Street'?"

If "Sesame Street" is to have an impact, the child must get to the television set; the program can have some impact on him once he is there. Since the program has no captive audience, it must address the first problem as well as the second. In the evaluation of "Sesame Street" this first problem was almost neglected. Fortunately, the producers of the program did not neglect it.

It is much more obvious in the case of "Sesame Street" than in the planned variation cases that it is necessary to measure implementation to determine effectiveness. To answer the question, "Does this program, as conceived, have an impact of a certain kind upon children?" it is important to ask as well, "Is this program, as conceived, implemented in the field, given certain kinds of instructions and teacher training?"

# Conference Participants

*with their affiliations at the time of the conference*

Bernard A. Banet  *High/Scope Educational Research Foundation*

C. Worth Bateman  *Urban Institute*

Joan Bissell  *Harvard University*

John E. Brandl  *University of Minnesota*

Marilyn B. Brewer  *Loyola University, Chicago*

David K. Cohen  *Harvard University*

James S. Coleman  *University of Chicago*

Lois-ellin Datta  *National Institute of Education*

Robert L. Egbert  *University of Nebraska*

Richard F. Elmore  *Harvard University*

Rashi Fein  *Harvard University*

Thomas K. Glennan  *National Institute of Education*

Milton Goldberg  *School District of Philadelphia*

Kermit Gordon  *Brookings Institution*

Robert W. Hartman  *Brookings Institution*

David N. Kershaw  *Mathematica, Inc.*

Carol VanDeusen Lukas  *Huron Institute*

Garry L. McDaniels  *National Institute of Education*

Frederick Mosteller  *Harvard University*

Guy H. Orcutt  *Yale University*

John Pincus  *Rand Corporation*

Alice M. Rivlin  *Brookings Institution*

Charles L. Schultze  *Brookings Institution*

**177**

Marshall S. Smith  *Harvard University*

Marian Sherman Stearns  *Stanford Research Institute*

P. Michael Timpane  *Brookings Institution*

Harold W. Watts  *University of Wisconsin*

David P. Weikart  *High/Scope Educational Research Foundation*

# Index

munity reaction to, 168; effects of, 82n–83n; federal support for, 4, 28, 47; financing of, 42. *See also* Planned variation experiments

Control groups: to evaluate education programs, 135, 138, 139, 140; for Follow Through, 32, 50–51; for HSPV, 95–96, 102

Cooley, William W., 136n

Crockett, Stanley, 8n

Cultural Linguistic Approach, 8

Culturally Democratic Learning Environment Model, 7

Curriculum: cognitive, 61–62; federal versus local decisions on, 16; Follow Through, 48–49, 101; HSPV, 86, 101, 105; planned variation research for, 72; preschool, 61–62, 101, 111; standardized tests to evaluate, 14, 15

Datta, Lois-ellin, 10n, 79, 81n, 85n, 111n, 149

Developmental program evaluation studies, 142–43

Di Lorenzo, Louis T., 88n

Disadvantaged children, 1; compensatory education programs for, 3, 4–5; long-term effects of preschool programs for, 82; models for specific needs of, 7

Dittmann, Laura L., 84n

Drill programs, 5, 108

Duncan, Beverly, 137n

Duncan, Dudley, 137

Dyer, J. L., 82n, 88n

Early education. *See* Preschool education

Economic Opportunity Act, 28, 29

EDC (Education Development Center) Open Education Program, 7, 10n, 111n, 143

Education. *See* Educational evaluation; Educational programs; Education system, elements of; Preschool education; Schools, effectiveness of

Educational evaluation, 23; through large-scale experiments, 24–26, 44–45, 145–46; measurements for, 72, 77, 130–32; problems in analyzing results of, 42–43, 143–46; validity of methods for, 129–32. *See also* Follow Through; Head Start Planned Variation; Planned variation experiments; Schools, effectiveness of; Standardized tests

Educational programs: external validity of, 131; implementation of, 131–32; internal validity of, 130–31; questionnaires to evaluate outcome of, 133–34; standardized tests to measure, 132–33; statistical significance of results of, 130–31

Educational Testing Service, 94

Education system, elements of, 127–29

Egbert, Robert L., 3n, 13n, 20n, 27, 28n, 33n, 37n

Elementary and Secondary Education Act, Title I, 42, 51, 57, 58, 168

Elmore, Richard F., 5n, 23, 155n

Emrick, John A., 33n

Enabler Model, 10, 93n, 102

Englemann-Becker Model, 10n, 144, 151; description of, 6, 118; results of, 108, 111n

Englemann, Siegfried, 6n, 35n

Environment, effect on child development, 83n

Erickson, Edsel L., 82n, 89n

Erlenbacher, Albert, 140n

Estes, Nolan, 23n

Evaluation. *See* Educational evaluation

Experimental Schools Program, 24

Featherman, David L., 137n

Featherstone, Helen, 109n, 110n

Federal government: criticism of educational programs sponsored by, 173; curriculum decisions by, 16; influence on local school systems, 25; role in planned variation experiments, 87–88, 90–91, 92, 94, 96; support for compensatory education, 4–5, 28, 47

Fillerup, Joseph M., 6n

Financing, of planned variation experiments: Follow Through, 27, 92–93, 167–68; HSPV, 90, 92–93, 107; by incentive grants, 42; by Title I assistance, 42

Flanagan, John C., 136n

Florida Parent Education Model, 7, 10n, 49, 102

Follow Through, 1; community reaction to, 20, 67–69, 168; compared with HSPV, 10–11, 26, 151; control groups for, 32, 50–51; coverage of, 25; curriculum, 48–49, 101; educational evaluation by, 23, 24, 26, 30, 37–38, 47, 53–54, 142; funding for, 27, 167–68; objectives of, 2, 12–13, 28, 149; origin of, 3, 4–5; parental role in, 5, 6, 7, 8, 26, 29, 59, 67, 68; policy constraints